KU-431-236

THE AWESOME POWER OF SLEEP

THE AWESOME POWER OF SLEEP

HOW SLEEP SUPER-CHARGES YOUR TEENAGE BRAIN

NICOLA MORGAN

WALKER
BOOKS

To Arthur, because in 12 years you'll be a teenager,
which should give you time to perfect your sleeping skills.
It's been wonderful having you to live with us during
lockdown but 4.30 a.m. is not what we call morning.

First published 2021 by Walker Books Ltd,
87 Vauxhall Walk, London SE11 5HJ

2 4 6 8 10 9 7 5 3 1

© 2021 Nicola Morgan

The right of Nicola Morgan to be identified as author of
this work has been asserted by her in accordance with the
Copyright, Designs and Patents Act 1988

This book has been typeset in Eureka Sans Pro

Printed in Great Britain by CPI Group (UK) Ltd, Croydon,
CR0 4YY

All rights reserved. No part of this book may be reproduced,
transmitted or stored in an information retrieval system in
any form or by any means, graphic, electronic or mechanical,
including photocopying, taping and recording, without prior
written permission from the publisher.

British Library Cataloguing in Publication Data: a catalogue
record for this book is available from the British Library

ISBN 978-1-4063-9540-2

www.walker.co.uk

CONTENTS ZZZZZ

INTRODUCTION

Do you sleep well? Fall asleep quickly when you turn your light off? Wake easily when your alarm rings? Spend the day feeling mostly wide awake? If so, lucky you! Very many people – adults and teenagers – say they don't get enough sleep and feel significantly tired during the day. It affects their well-being and performance in every area of life.

Everyone experiences occasional bad nights or phases when sleep seems difficult, but certain groups of people have more problems than others: teenagers and people under stress, for example. So, if you're a teenager *and* under stress, you have a double chance of sleep problems. And that's not only distressing but also undermines your well-being and how you feel and function during the day.

More and more people are starting to take note of the science that tells us how important adequate sleep is to our mental and physical health. **The trouble is that when we can't sleep, worrying about the importance of sleep is likely to keep us awake!** We need to find a balance: we must believe in the power of sleep without panicking about not getting enough. This book aims to help you.

The Awesome Power of Sleep unpicks the up-to-date science. You will discover how sleep affects physical and mental health, including emotion, mood, memory, appetite and weight. You'll learn the effects of daytime napping, late-night revision, travelling across time zones, anxiety, exercise, caffeine, light, screens (including ebook readers), sleeping pills, melatonin, reading before bed, temperature, routines, weekend lie-ins and sleeping too much. Be prepared to be fascinated by the research into how sleep helps us learn and remember, including ways we may be able to time learning and sleep for the best effects.

Then there's the fascinating world of dreaming! What's it for? Do dreams mean anything? Have you ever been in a dream and known you're dreaming? And have you even been able to control your dreams? Join the club of lucid dreamers!

All the science would be pointless without strategies for better sleep. This book gives you all the strategies and solutions you need, based on science. You'll be able to analyse your own sleep and discover what you could be doing better. You'll find tips you can use throughout your life. Some will work better for you than others: try them all and do what works.

Unfortunately, some people think it's cool to manage on little sleep. This can include some students during the time leading up to exams. I confess that I used to boast about how little sleep I was having and thought this meant I was working hard. I made myself ill, which wasn't cool and didn't help my results at all.

I wasn't always a healthy sleeper and I didn't always prioritise sleep as I do now. But I've learnt the real benefits that come when I get the best sleep I can. I travel a lot, including overseas trips with major time differences, jet lag and sleeping in hotels, but I have to make sure my brain is in top condition. Add to that the fact that I'm naturally a stressy person and you have someone at risk of poor sleep. But simple strategies and routines make sure I almost always get the best sleep possible in those difficult conditions. And when my tricks don't work, I don't panic, because I know that a bad night here or there isn't a problem.

AN EXTRA TEENAGE PROBLEM

In some ways sleep is the same for anyone but there are factors that are especially relevant to adolescents – anyone from the age of around eleven or twleve until well into their twenties. You.

First, the most common reasons for not getting to sleep easily are anxiety or a brain that won't go quiet. Although adults have

8

the same trouble, teenagers have less practice in an important skill: diverting thoughts away from worry. The part of the brain we need to control and regulate our emotions and reactions is the prefrontal cortex. It's the last part of the brain to develop and doesn't finish doing so until well into your twenties. So, you are at a disadvantage compared to adults when it comes to controlling dark, scary, negative thoughts. (Adults often aren't great at it either.)

Add the fact that teenage brains need more sleep than adults, as you'll discover on page 69. And that you have to get up early for school and do schoolwork in the evenings.

Finally, add the reality that teenagers are highly social and often need to be connected to each other via screens – screens which strongly interfere with sleep.

That all adds up to a massive problem: lots of sleep-deprived young people who feel terrible during the day and whose well-being and performance are likely to be damaged.

Fortunately, the solutions are all in this book. Even with teenage pressures and brain changes that affect sleep patterns, you can become super-charged by sleep. **So much of the science is new and your parents and teachers may not know it.** Share it with them! Often when I visit schools, I find myself giving detailed sleep counselling to teachers. I'm shocked at the bad habits many adults have, while telling teenagers how to behave!

THE TRUTH IS CLEAR

We all need enough sleep to have the best health. We need to believe in its importance and then learn how to get it. This book will help you have a healthy, unproblematic relationship with sleep. Then the hours when your head is on your pillow can do their job of making your brain and body the best they can be.

CHAPTER ONE:
YOU AND SLEEP

This chapter is all about you! You'll be able to assess your own sleep, see whether you have any specific sleep problems and find out what you already know, before we move to the awesome science of sleep. Everyone is different, with a whole range of different behaviours, habits and problems. When we're trying to get to sleep, we are very alone in our own heads and we often don't know how that fits with other people's experiences. This section helps you put yourself in context. It's the beginning of your journey towards great sleep.

The Awesome Power of Sleep has activities, quizzes and things to think about, so it would be great if you had a notebook or just used a computer or app for recording your answers, thoughts and ideas.

QUIZ: TESTING YOUR KNOWLEDGE NOW

This is to test what you know now, so that you can see what you learn through the book. Don't worry if you don't know any of the answers! One of the learning techniques we know works is called "pre-testing", where you test yourself before learning. The main benefit of this is that, as you start to read the material, it will feel slightly familiar and your brain will be triggered to focus on the information as being important.

Test the adults you know, too!

1. What does REM in REM sleep stand for?

2. Does deep non-dreaming sleep typically happen mostly in the first half or second half of the night?

3. What is a hypnagogic myoclonic twitch?

4. At night, should your bedroom be a bit colder or a bit warmer than during the day?

5. Are there some animals that don't sleep?

6. Do other animals (i.e. non-humans) dream?

7. Is it true that some people are biologically more wakeful in the morning and others at night, or is this difference just about habit?

8. Can teenage sleeping habits mostly be explained by a mixture of laziness and looking at screens late at night?

9. If you sleep badly before an exam, does this mean you are certain to do less well in the exam?

10. If you have a test on Tuesday afternoon, is it best to learn the material during the day on Monday, late on Monday night or on Tuesday morning?

11. If someone is screaming and thrashing their arms about while they're asleep, should you wake them?

12. Does exercise help or hinder night-time sleep?

13. If you dream about doing something violent or horrible, does this mean you are a violent or horrible person?

14. Which three of these things in the late evening are most likely to negatively affect sleep: a warm bath, a milky drink, alcohol, going for a run or other sport, herbal tea, yoga, checking your phone messages.

Check the answers on page 177! By the end of this book, you will know all that and much, much more. Try the test again at the end!

QUIZ: HOW WELL DO YOU SLEEP?

This quiz is designed to show you where you are now with your sleep and whether you have enough or not. Your answers might change from day to day, week to week or month to month so you can do this quiz as many times as you want. If you answer based on last night's sleep, your answers are just relevant to that and might be very different if you answered on another day. Do this quiz in the afternoon or evening, answering for last night and how you feel today. Record today's date so that you can look back at this later.

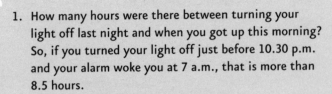

1. How many hours were there between turning your light off last night and when you got up this morning? So, if you turned your light off just before 10.30 p.m. and your alarm woke you at 7 a.m., that is more than 8.5 hours.

   a. More than 8.5 hours.
   b. Between 7 and 8.5 hours.
   c. Between 6 and 7 hours.
   d. Fewer than 6 hours.

2. Roughly how long did it take you to go to sleep last night?

   a. I fell asleep very quickly.
   b. I'd guess maybe 10–20 minutes or so.
   c. More than 25 minutes.

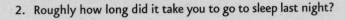

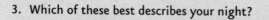

3. **Which of these best describes your night?**

    a. I slept pretty well and didn't spend much time awake.
    b. I woke several times but was able to get back to sleep fairly quickly.
    c. I slept badly, with a lot of time awake and feeling stressed.

4. **Do you often struggle to fall asleep?**

    a. Yes, often.
    b. Sometimes but not often.
    c. No, very rarely or never.

5. **Do you often wake much earlier than you need to and have difficulty getting back to sleep?**

    a. Yes, often.
    b. Somtimes but not often.
    c. No, very rarely or never.

6. **Would you say sleep is generally a problem for you? Select the answer you agree with the most.**

    a. Not a problem.
    b. Occasionally or a slight problem.
    c. Quite often a problem or quite a big problem.
    d. A big problem.

7. **How sleepy were you during yesterday or today? Select the answer which describes you most accurately.**

    a. I was fine during the day yesterday but started feeling very sleepy at about 7 p.m. and for the rest of the evening.
    b. I felt sleepy this morning but was OK after that.
    c. I felt sleepy for a while after lunch but was OK otherwise.
    d. I didn't feel sleepy.

8. What other things did you notice during the day? Select all that significantly apply.

   a. Difficulty concentrating.
   b. Feeling irritable, snappy or moody.
   c. Feeling tearful and emotional.
   d. Being forgetful or making simple mistakes.
   e. Being clumsy.
   f. None of these things.

9. In each of these A/B pairs, select the one you more strongly agree with; if you really can't decide, put a question mark.

   A. I think I'm generally a bad sleeper.
   B. I think I'm generally a good sleeper, though I have occasional bad phases.

   A. I think sleep is very important and I worry I don't get enough.
   B. I know sleep is very important but I'm not worried because I think I get enough.

   A. I often feel very sleepy during the day and struggle to stay awake in class.
   B. I usually feel quite alert through the day but I'll feel tired by the evening.

   A. It's common for me to get less than 6 hours of sleep a night.
   B. It would be very unusual for me to get less than 6 hours.

   A. I most often get less than 7.5 hours of sleep a night (7 if adult).
   B. I most often get more than 7.5 hours (7 if adult).

A. I don't think I get enough sleep and I'd feel better if I had more.
B. I think I get enough sleep for me because I feel OK during the day.

A. I find it extremely hard to get up when my alarm goes and feel significantly sleepy for at least two hours.
B. When my alarm (or adult) wakes me up, I feel quite awake fairly quickly.

A. At weekends or holidays, I often/always sleep in for hours.
B. At weekends or holidays, I occasionally/never sleep in for hours or I have a small lie-in.

HOW TO SCORE

1. Score 3 points for a or b; 1 for c; 0 for d.

2. Score 2 points for a; 3 for b; 0 for c. (Falling asleep immediately can be either a sign of being relaxed or a sign of not having enough sleep.)

3. Score 3 for a; 2 for b; 0 for c.

4. Score 0 for a; 2 for b; 3 for c.

5. Score 0 for a; 2 for b; 3 for c.

6. Score 3 for a; 2 for b; 1 for c; 0 for d.

7. Score 0 for a and b; 2 for c; 3 for d.

8. Score 0 for a–e; 3 for f.

9. Score 0 for every A answer; 2 for every B answer. If you can't decide between the statements, score 1.

HOW TO INTERPRET YOUR SCORE

The maximum score on this quiz is 40, and the higher your score the better your current relationship with sleep. The lower your score, the more chance you may have some negative sleep patterns or a difficult relationship with sleep. When we sleep well – or have the right amount of sleep for our individual needs – we find it fairly painless to wake to our alarm, fall asleep easily without lying awake feeling anxious, don't experience much sleepiness during the day and feel positive towards the idea of sleep in general.

But note that many of the things that might have brought your score down can be very temporary and can also be caused by other things such as stress about exams, minor and routine illness or upsetting things going on in your life, such as moving school or house or worries about family or friends.

Nevertheless, this score is important as a guideline to how your sleep is right now. The aim of this book is to raise your score to the best it can be and to give you the tools to avoid bad sleep patterns later, even if they are perfect right now.

START A SLEEP DIARY

Anyone who wants to improve their sleep would benefit from starting a sleep diary. If you ever consult a doctor about sleep problems, they will probably ask you to keep one. This way, you can start to see patterns between certain activities or situations and better or worse sleep. You will find templates online but you can use the one on the next page to base yours on. Use your notebook or do it on-screen. Or you could use them simply as ideas to create your own.

If you start your diary now, you'll soon be able to put into practice the things you learn and also see what effects those strategies have.

If you wear a sleep tracking device, this will give you a record of when you fell asleep and woke up, as well as time you spent in dream sleep and in light or deep sleep. They are not always accurate so don't become obsessed by analysing your results!

However, these devices are not cheap and you certainly do not need one. They don't help you sleep – they are just a tool for measuring your sleep. And some people find they actually hinder sleep because you can become obsessed by measurements instead of just acting sensibly and healthily during the evenings.

HOW TO USE YOUR DIARY

Fill it in for at least a week. If any questions don't apply, ignore them. While filling in the answers, try to think whether something might be relevant to your sleep success but record it even if you don't believe it's relevant. (You might start seeing some surprising patterns.)

When you've done this for at least a week – or when you have had some variety in your nights – start to look at your answers and see if you can detect any patterns. Do you sleep better or worse after certain things?

It's very possible that you won't detect the patterns after only a week. Keep up with your recording but don't worry if you sometimes forget. Once you've read Chapters Eight and Nine you'll see some more things to look out for and everything will start to fall into place. You might even have a "light-bulb moment" and suddenly realise what it is that stops you having a great night.

Morning

Day of week:	M	T	W	T	F	S	S
Last night I turned my light out at:							
I fell asleep: • Quickly • After a short while • After a long time							
During the night: (record e.g. whether I woke often/couldn't get back to sleep etc.)							
Anything that disturbed my sleep: (e.g. noise; feelings; discomfort)							
I got up this morning at:							
I slept around how many hours?							
During the hour after I woke up this morning, I felt:							

Evening

Day of week:	M	T	W	T	F	S	S
How many caffeinated drinks I drank from 2 p.m. onwards:							
I did very energetic exercise (e.g. sport, run, gym, dance) in the morning/afternoon/after school:							
I did gentle exercise (e.g. walk, yoga, stretches) in the morning/afternoon/after school:							
Anything that happened today which was either very exciting or very stressful/upsetting/worrying:							
My general mood today – from very positive/relaxed to very negative/anxious:							
I did these things during the 2 hours before turning my light off: · Exercise that raised my heart rate · Watched TV/film/video · Used social media/texting · Had an argument or was very annoyed/upset · Drank coffee or other caffeinated drink (including ordinary tea) · Did schoolwork							

Now you're all set to get the most out of this book and use it as a real tool for healthy sleep. You have started to understand how important and wonderful sleep is and you've got an idea of how much of a problem it is or isn't for you. Let's look at the very cool up-to-date science of what is going on in your brain and body during the hours of darkness and let's get ready to super-charge you with the awesome power of sleep.

CHAPTER TWO:
INTRODUCING SLEEP SCIENCE

In this chapter, you'll discover loads of facts about the science of sleep: what it is, why we need it, what makes it happen when it does, how much you need and the ways in which our sleep behaviours are different. If you skip this and just go straight to the strategies, it will be like following some rules without understanding why. I think "why" is very important!

SUPER-CHARGED SLEEP FACT
OPPORTUNITY, LENGTH, LATENCY AND ARCHITECTURE

- How long we give ourselves between turning the light off and our morning alarm is sleep **"opportunity"**
- How long it takes to get to sleep is sleep **"latency"**
- How long we actually spend asleep is sleep **"length"**
- The pattern of our sleep stages through the night is our sleep **"architecture"**.

WHAT IS SLEEP FOR?

If we don't know *why* sleep is important, we might not fully believe it is; we might try to find ways to manage on less; we might well not take it seriously. Knowing what it's for, what it does to our bodies and brains and what lack of it does, helps us prioritise it. And it's interesting, too!

Not all scientists agree on everything, whether to do with sleep or other complex topics. Some of the science of sleep is new and some of it needs to be researched further before we can feel sure of it. Sleep is often very hard to investigate as there are so many other life factors that could be affecting the results of any research. I have tried to use only the conclusions that the big health or academic organisations quote and to listen to scientists who have been researching this field for a long time. But even they can be wrong: sometimes scientists – like anyone – can be blinkered by their passion for the subject. And initial findings can be contradicted by someone else using a different method or examining a different group of people.

SUPER-CHARGED SLEEP FACT
LIMITS OF RESEARCH

News headlines and research results are often misleading: for example, a headline might say "Scientists discover that dreaming improves problem-solving skills". What you might not realise is that the study involved only a tiny number of people and that the method was to wake them up during different sleep stages and ask them to solve a particular puzzle. All research studies need to be replicated many times before one can be sure that the result is generally likely to be true. Researchers have to work hard to avoid being biased, seeing what they want to see, or missing some other factor that is skewing the results. Not all research is as good as others and it's often hard to distinguish. Newspapers and news websites also want to attract readers, so a headline often has that motive, rather than scientific accuracy.

Let's check out how today's experts believe sleep directly affects our health and lives. Most of these points will be discussed more fully when I talk about the relevant sleep stage for each. See which ones you've noticed for yourself.

LEARNING AND MEMORY

- **Learning and processing information** – You'll find more about this when I talk about schoolwork and exams from page 83.

- **Memory** – Forming new memories and recalling old ones – again, more detail from page 83. This is very relevant at your age, as you are learning so much new information for schoolwork and exams, but we learn new things at every stage of life so we all want to keep our memory as strong as possible.

EMOTIONAL HEALTH

- **Emotions, mood and mental health** – Sleep seems to be very important in processing negative events and dealing with the emotions from them. In terms of general mood, you know that after a bad night you typically feel "out of sorts", low, grumpy, negative. Just as sleep affects daily mood, it can also affect mental health problems such as depression. More on page 107.

- **Self-control and regulation of behaviour and decisions** – We are more likely to be able to control our impulses and make rational decisions when we've had good sleep. This includes impulses such as eating more sugary or fatty things than we know we should; being aggressive or violent or merely snappy; or taking risks with activities such as gambling. In short, we tend to be more impulsive and less controlled after poor sleep.

- **Stress** – While we sleep, our stress levels reduce (along with blood pressure). Separately, during the day we can feel anxious about the poor sleep we've just had or the poor sleep we think we're about to have: this makes us more likely to struggle to get to sleep.

PHYSICAL HEALTH

- **Cardiac health and blood pressure** – Sleep lowers blood pressure, which helps keep our heart and arteries healthy. Research[1] from as long ago as 1996 showed that even a small sleep loss among healthy, fit people raised blood pressure the following day. Raised blood pressure over a long period of time raises the risk of heart attacks and strokes.

- **Gut health** – Digestion, stress and sleep are intricately linked and research suggests that the links are in all directions, with sleep affecting digestion and digestion affecting sleep, for example.

- **Regulation of the hormone insulin, which controls blood glucose levels** – A few nights in a row of poor sleep can noticeably affect blood glucose levels. Sleep regulates other hormones, too, keeping your whole body's metabolism on track. Diabetes, a condition where people don't produce insulin properly, may be affected by poor sleep. This is only the case for the Type 2 form of diabetes, which is lifestyle related. Type 1 diabetes is not lifestyle related.

- **Immune system** – Preventing illnesses, whether minor or more serious. You'll often find you get more colds and minor bugs when you're tired. More seriously, various cancers are more common in shift workers[2] (a group of people commonly studied because their sleep patterns are very different from people working regular hours) and this is also shown in animal studies.

- **Growth and repair** – Growth hormone is produced during sleep and this works to repair damaged cells as well as helping you grow at a normal rate.

- **Weight** – People who sleep less tend to have more problems keeping within their healthy weight ranges.[3] You'd think that getting up early would mean you're burning more energy but that is more than offset by the impact on the behaviour of your hunger and fullness hormones, your metabolism (how quickly your body burns energy) and likely food choices. Remember the point above about poor sleep leading to less self-control? It's been shown in many studies that after a bad night's sleep people are likely to consume more calories and make more unhealthy choices. The hunger hormone (ghrelin) and fullness hormone (leptin) are regulated by sleep, so lack of sleep can lead to people feeling more hungry and not feeling full. Lack of sleep also makes it harder to exercise willpower which can result in people being more likely to choose higher-calorie foods. (Please note that a healthy diet includes every type of food and there is nothing wrong at all with eating a certain amount of fatty, sugary or salty foods. You should not think about calorie contents of individual foods but aim to eat what feels like a nutritious, varied, enjoyable diet.)

HOUSEKEEPING IN YOUR BRAIN!

While you're awake, your brain is taking in vast amounts of information, creating connections and pathways between brain cells, trying and often failing to become skilled at a whole load of actions. It is also creating a lot of waste: broken connections, faulty pathways, dead cells, and proteins. During sleep, particularly deep sleep, the spaces between brain cells open up, becoming broader. And through these channels flows fluid called cerebrospinal fluid, or CSF, washing away all the waste.

This system, which was only discovered in 2012, is called the glymphatic system. You may have heard of the lymphatic system of glands that go throughout your body carrying "lymph", a fluid that fights infections by removing toxins and producing antibodies. When you have swollen glands under your jaw during a throat infection, for example, these are your lymph glands working to fight that infection. The glymphatic system has a similar role but just in the brain and spinal cord: your "central nervous system".

CSF flows through your central nervous system all the time but the flow is greater during deep sleep and the glymphatic system itself is far more active during sleep than wakefulness. It's estimated that the spaces between brain cells increase by up to 60 per cent during deep sleep, allowing this to happen. Scientists also believe that during waking hours our brain just has too much going on and can't perform this clean-up function. A bit like a busy school with the cleaners only able to do their work after hours because otherwise the corridors and rooms are too full of rushing people.

IN SHORT

You can see that sleep has a vast range of functions. So many reasons for prioritising it! It is a wonderful, nourishing medicine and entirely free. It super-charges your brain.

AN IMPORTANT REASSURANCE

If you are someone who often sleeps badly or you are going through a poor sleep phase right now, you might feel worried and anxious about all the health benefits you could be missing.

Here are reasons not to worry:

- Most of them are very long-term effects, and the negatives will not occur just because you're having a few weeks or months of bad sleep.
- They are only statistical likelihoods, not certainties.
- Most poor sleep phases are just that: phases. They vanish.
- There are many other life factors which contribute towards your health: your diet, exercise, social interactions, fresh air, sunlight and all the other ways in which you can take care of yourself. Sleep is only one part of health.
- Most importantly, there are lots of things you'll be able to do to improve your sleep, now and over your whole life. It's never too late to start sleeping better and getting immediate benefits.

That's what this book is for: to arm you with strategies for a life of the best sleep you can get. And to help you not to worry when you can't.

SUPER-BUSTED SLEEP MYTH
SLEEP IS MAINLY FOR REST AND RE-ENERGISING

We used to think this because we didn't really have evidence about anything else. But now we know so much more. Matthew Walker, one of the world's leading sleep experts, says[4] that "results of thousands of studies" show that there are no "biological functions that do not benefit by a good night's sleep."

HOW MUCH SLEEP DO WE NEED?

Everyone's needs are different. Some of those differences are age-related but there's also great variance between individuals.

Everything you'll read about this is based on averages. These averages are based on many years of research into people all around the world, people of different ages and in different situations. This means that it's worth believing the averages while also remembering that not everyone falls in the middle of an average range, of course. Averages are ways of working out middles or norms, but some people will always be at the edges.

Another important factor when thinking about how much sleep we might need is that there are two main methods scientists use to study this. One is to see how long people naturally sleep when no alarm wakes them up. The other is to only allow people certain amounts of sleep and measure how their performance, behaviour or health suffers or improves, in a wide variety of ways. Such studies will typically split the subjects into groups, giving each group different amounts of sleep or waking them up at certain stages of sleep and then testing mental or other functions.

Those are two very different measurements. How long I might sleep if nothing woke me tomorrow morning, and how early you could wake me without me suffering, could be widely different times.

Also, for that first measurement – looking at how long people sleep when not woken – some of this research looks at groups such as tribes living a hunter-gatherer existence in South America or Africa, regulating their days by the seasons, weather and culture. But this won't tell us what human bodies "need", only what those groups of people allow themselves. There are a number of reasons why they might typically sleep the amount that they do. It doesn't prove one way or another this is the ideal length of sleep for humans.

A study in Finland in 2014 had an interesting method: it looked at 3000 people and measured the amount they slept against how many days of sick leave they took. The researchers noticed that for the least amount of sick leave, women needed 7.63 hours and men needed 7.76 hours of sleep a night. But one study doesn't usually prove anything. News headlines tend to refer to a single study and often make the story sound more clear-cut and dramatic than it usually is. We need to add the studies together and think carefully how we interpret them.

However, based on all the vast amount of research we have, **it's reasonable to say that adults generally do better and feel better when they have a sleep opportunity of seven to eight hours and adolescents (eleven to mid-twenties) when they have more than eight hours. I'll say a bit more about this difference when I talk about special teenage sleep patterns on page 69.**

Some people do seem to need more and some manage on a bit less.

SUPER-CHARGED SLEEP FACT
SLEEP DEPRIVATION RECORDS

A forced lack of sleep is regarded as so dangerous that Guinness World Records no longer recognises attempts to set a record for the longest time spent awake. The last world record was held by seventeen-year-old Randy Gardner with 11 days 25 minutes, though there are several claims to have exceeded that. When people try to go without sleep entirely, within only a few days severe and distressing symptoms set in, including mood changes, inability to focus, psychotic behaviour and hallucinations. Animals deprived of sleep display very disturbing symptoms and die faster than if deprived of food. For these reasons, any attempt to try to break a record is dangerous and irresponsible.

Note that there is a huge difference between a phase of not being able to sleep (insomnia) and deliberately forcing a lack of sleep. Periods of not being able to sleep are common, as this book shows, and something you should not worry about but just learn how to improve.

CAN SOME PEOPLE REALLY MANAGE ON VERY LITTLE SLEEP?

You might have heard stories of people – usually world or business leaders – who claim to manage perfectly on as little as four or five hours' sleep a night. British Prime Minister Margaret Thatcher and US President Ronald Reagan are two frequently-cited examples. However, there are three things you need to consider:

1. It's likely that in those cases (and in other cases where people claim to manage on little sleep) they were exaggerating, boasting in the belief that managing on little sleep was somehow praiseworthy.

2. No tests were done on them to measure either how much sleep they were really getting or whether their abilities or health were actually affected by having less than the recommended sleep.

3. Both Thatcher and Reagan developed Alzheimer's, which many scientists believe may sometimes be linked to a long history of very little sleep.

However, there may be very rare instances of people who are genuinely able to do very well on very little sleep. Scientists have identified at least one genetic mutation related to this, known as DEC2[5]. People with this will naturally wake up at around 4 a.m. after going to bed at midnight, and are full of energy, alert and ready to work. Even if they have the opportunity to sleep longer, they just don't. Perhaps Margaret Thatcher and Ronald Reagan did have this gene, but we will never know.

Sleep scientist David Dinges is so sure of the unlikelihood of maintaining good mental function on less than six hours a night on a regular basis that he has issued a challenge to anyone who thinks they can. No one has succeeded so far. Dinges estimates that the number of people with this ability is closer to zero per cent than one per cent and that it is genetic and cannot be learnt. So, no, you can't train yourself to work well on little sleep.

SUPER-CHARGED SLEEP TIP
DON'T BOAST ABOUT LACK OF SLEEP

"Sleep is for wimps – I don't need as much as you" is a dangerous attitude which both exam students and people in work can display, a kind of macho attitude. Sleeping well is no more a sign of weakness than eating good food or taking daily exercise. Sleep is necessary and important: don't try to manage on less of it! You'll work better if you sleep better.

DOES NAPPING MAKE UP FOR POOR SLEEP? WILL A POWER NAP HELP?

People nap for two main reasons. One is when they are very tired during the day and feel a powerful need to sleep; this often happens when we aren't well. The other is a more deliberate attempt to improve work-rate by having a nap before going back to work.

The latter type of strategic short sleep is often called a

"power nap". There's a range of evidence that it might help in certain circumstances and with certain types of task.

Going for a short sleep if you feel overwhelmingly tired during the day won't do you any harm at all and may indeed make you better able to work afterwards; doing it too much or too often is likely to shorten your night-time sleep and it's that night-time sleep you really need. If you do have a day-time nap, there are two things to watch out for:

1. Don't do it in the evening, as this will disrupt your night-time sleep.

2. Don't wait till you're exhausted: if you're someone who tends to feel sleepy during the afternoon or if you know you're going to miss some sleep tonight, nap *before* the tiredness sets in. That way, you won't fall too deeply asleep and wake up groggy. Research into long-distance pilots suggests that napping at the start of their flight has a better effect than napping later, when the pilot is actually tired. Further research has confirmed that early naps have a better effect on later concentration, even though these naps may be lighter sleep than the sleep we get when we are really tired.[6]

So, it's a mixture of yes and no: a nap might help in some circumstances but not if it affects your night-time sleep.

All sleep is good but night-time sleep should be our top priority, whether or not we also nap!

WHAT MAKES US SLEEP WHEN WE DO?

Understanding this is at the very heart of how we can sleep better. Two separate processes in our body drive us towards night-time sleep.

1. SLEEP PRESSURE

From the moment we wake in the morning, sleep pressure builds gradually and inevitably until we fall asleep that night. If we have a nap, that sleep pressure is temporarily and partially relieved but a nap does not replace our night-time sleep. The sleep pressure mounts again immediately after the nap.

This biological process is part of "homeostasis", a system whereby the brain regulates various aspects of our body, including temperature, appetite, hormones and sleepiness versus wakefulness. In the case of sleep/wake homeostasis, this seems to be mainly controlled by the chemical adenosine, which is produced in the brain. As soon as we wake in the morning, adenosine starts to build. The longer we are awake, the higher our adenosine levels and the more we need to sleep. During sleep, adenosine drops and continues to drop the longer we are asleep.

The need for sleep that adenosine creates is sometimes called a "sleep debt": you only lose the debt once you've paid it off by sleeping.

Caffeine and other stimulants – such as energy drinks – block the effect of adenosine by disrupting its work in the brain. Caffeine also increases levels of the stress chemical, adrenaline, in the body.

Sleep pressure is mainly a drive towards deep sleep, rather than light sleep or dream sleep. We know this because when we lose sleep over a few nights, when we next get the chance to sleep for a whole night, we will have more *deep* sleep than usual, compared to the other stages of sleep. Deep sleep is especially important for rest and re-energising.

So far, so simple: the longer you're awake, the more you'll need to go to sleep. But it isn't that simple...

2. CIRCADIAN RHYTHM – OUR BODY CLOCK

This is the second process that regulates night-time sleep and daytime wakefulness. It involves a special area of the brain and a hormone called melatonin.

Inside your brain, you have a group of cells, sometimes called your "body clock" but technically called the "suprachiasmatic nucleus" or SCN. It consists of about 20,000 cells, which is tiny in relation to the 80–100 billion nerve cells or "neurons", as well as billions of other cells in your brain.

SUPER-CHARGED SLEEP FACT
YOU HAVE TWO BODY CLOCKS

Because the human brain has two linked halves – the left and right hemispheres – almost every brain part is duplicated, though the left and right are not *exactly* the same. So, you have two SCNs, each of around 10,000 cells, each positioned slightly to one side of the centre of your forehead, immediately behind the eyes. It needs to be there because it reacts to daylight – even when your eyes are shut. Any deeper inside your brain and it wouldn't detect the changing light.

Every evening, mostly corresponding to daylight fading, the SCN triggers the release of melatonin. Melatonin is often called the "sleep hormone" but it doesn't directly make you sleepy.

Melatonin *prepares* your body for sleep, starting around two hours before you'll actually fall asleep. It prompts your body to start various changes that make sleep likely. And every morning, mostly corresponding to daylight starting, the same SCN triggers melatonin to switch off and prepare your body to wake up, all fresh and alert for the day.

The fact that this happens each day at roughly the same

time (even though in countries far from the Equator day and night happen at different times depending on the time of year) is why this is called a circadian rhythm: "circa" is Latin for "approximately" and "diem" is Latin for "day". All animals, including humans, have circadian rhythms that fit well with the 24-hour day – but don't exactly match. The human circadian cycle is more like 24 and a quarter hours, but there are age differences, with adolescents and people in their twenties having a typical cycle of 26–28 hours and much older adults a shorter one. But we don't notice the difference between our body clock and the actual Earth's day because each day our internal system resets according to daylight, alarm clocks and all our daily routines that rule when we wake or sleep.

WHEN DOES MELATONIN SWITCH ON AND OFF?

The timing is affected by two main things:

1. **Darkness/daylight** – Because humans are night-time sleepers, our melatonin naturally switches on as darkness falls. Morning daylight being detected by our SCN helps trigger melatonin to switch off, so that we can become awake. Sometimes melatonin is called the darkness hormone rather than the sleep hormone. In fact, the "mela" part of the word means "black" or "dark".

    This helps explain several things you might have noticed:

    ★ If you live in a country far north of the Equator, it's often harder to fall asleep during summer months, because it stays light for longer, and harder to wake up on winter mornings, because it's still dark outside. If you live in a country far south of the Equator, the opposite is the case. If you live near the Equator, where there's not much difference between the amount of darkness and daylight from one season to the next, you won't notice.

★ If your curtains or blinds are thin, you'll often wake earlier in the morning as it gets light outside.

★ If you have to wake up very early, you'll feel groggy even if you went to sleep earlier. This is because your melatonin levels are likely to be high as it's still dark and your body is in sleep mode.

★ Our biological need for rhythms of night and day is severely disturbed by travel across time zones. If you take a long-distance flight to a very different time zone, you'll feel confused, dizzy and groggy until your circadian rhythms have got used to the new pattern. (By which time you probably have to go home, when you'll feel groggy all over again...)

It also helps explain what I'll look at on page 56: that if you don't go to sleep until the early hours of the morning, you'll go straight into a pattern typical for the second half of the night, rather than a normal sleep pattern: your brain recognises that this is the end of the night, not the beginning.

2. **Other routines** – The brain is very strongly affected by routines and patterns, so your daily routine of meals and activities during the day, and particularly during the evening, will help tell your brain when it's time to sleep. (This is going to be extremely helpful when we get to strategies for sleeping better and falling asleep earlier!)

SUPER-CHARGED SLEEP FACT
THE BODY CLOCK IN BLIND PEOPLE

Because circadian rhythms are mostly regulated by daylight
hitting light receptors behind the eyes, when blind people
have no light perception at all, they often have trouble finding
a 24-hour circadian rhythm and may have problems with
sleep patterns and suffer excessive sleepiness during the day.
However, when other daily routines are used, such as having the
same meal and exercise times each day, a typical human sleep/
wake pattern can happen. Also, the majority of people classified
as blind do have some light perception and are more likely to
have the same circadian rhythms as sighted people.

When people don't have a 24-hour sleep/wake cycle that
brings sleep during darkness and wakefulness during daylight,
this is called "Non 24-Hour Sleep Wake Disorder", or sometimes
just Non-24. It's estimated that around 70 per cent of people
with no light perception suffer from this, as well as a very small
number of sighted people. Expert intervention helps, which
may include melatonin medication and will certainly include
creating strong routines.

TYPICAL AGE DIFFERENCES

There are also some age differences in when we feel sleepy.

- **Babies up to around eighteen months** – Newborn
  babies sleep around sixteen hours a day but not all in one
  go. Unborn babies sleep even longer and premature babies
  tend to sleep as they would if they were still in the womb.
  Newborns take a while to get into a night-time sleeping
  habit. When they are able to go longer between feeds, if
  parents try to create a different routine between day and

night, babies fairly quickly move towards sleeping more at night than during the day.

- **Young children up to about the age of ten** – After about the age of three years, children will usually have all their sleep at night, perhaps having a nap if they are particularly tired.

- **Teenagers and young adults** – For reasons we don't fully understand, adolescent body clocks switch melatonin on late at night, around the time or even later than when adults typically feel sleepy. This means it can be hard for teenagers to go to sleep and get the hours they need before school. I'll talk much more about this in the section on teenage sleep.

- **Adults from late twenties to sixties or seventies** – Circadian rhythms mean sleepiness comes any time from 10.30–11.30 and waking up for an alarm seven to eight hours later is usually easily managed.

- **Elderly adults** – Biological sleep needs are less (though many older people do sleep long hours) and older people often naturally wake early in the morning. They may have greater sleep pressure because energy loss may be greater during the day, but melatonin levels decrease as we get older, which can explain why some elderly people have difficulty sleeping at night as much as they'd like but do more often have daytime naps.

Everything I've said so far has been about averages. It doesn't take into account individual differences caused by factors such as habits (good or bad); lifestyle needs such as shift-work, or a very early start for a long journey to school or work, or a caring role; or whether you are naturally an "owl" or a "lark".

SUPER-CHARGED SLEEP FACT
HUMANS AND "BIPHASIC SLEEP"

Have you read that humans are naturally wired to have a two-phase (biphasic) night-time sleep, waking in the middle of the night and getting up to do things, or even socialising? We do not know if this is true. We know that some societies have done this but we don't have evidence that this is "something humans are wired to do". It's likely to have been a cultural habit, not a biological one. Now that we can look at people who live in communities without electricity, including people who live a largely hunter-gatherer life and set their daily patterns by the sun and stars, we can see that the most common human practice is to have a long night-time sleep, though in some cultures there's also a shorter day-time nap. It makes sense for humans to be asleep during hours of darkness, because our eyesight is not good during this time.

On the other hand, humans *may* naturally be biphasic, but only when you consider the whole 24-hour period, not just night-time. Many cultures, including modern tribes that live without electricity, have an afternoon sleep. In modern industrialised countries we have largely had to stop this afternoon nap because we are obsessed with getting a lot of work done. Very many people feel sleepy in the afternoon, which may be at least partly to do with the effect of eating, but is also in part due to our melatonin levels and circadian rhythms.

And you'll know that some societies do have a long lunch or break from work during the day. Spain, as an obvious example, has the "siesta", a period of several hours when many businesses and shops will be closed before re-opening again during the evening. Many people sleep during part of this time.

So, yes, humans may be naturally biphasic but probably not in our night-time sleep. We may just have two phases of natural sleep, the main one at night and a smaller one in the afternoon.

Or it could be that those societies that have two sleeps have just adopted this as something that suits their climate and system of work and society.

Humans are not only the product of our biology (nature) but also of our environment and cultures (nurture).

OWLS AND LARKS - CHRONOTYPES

For a long time, humans have noticed that some people seem to operate better and feel more alert in the early mornings, finding it quite easy to wake up with their alarm clocks and feeling bright and awake quickly. Meanwhile, others seem to be more alert and productive in the evenings and find it really hard to wake up when they need to for school or work. Some people used to think that these differences were all down to habit and maybe personality. People who found it hard to wake up in the mornings were sometimes accused of simply being lazy or told that they should go to bed earlier and then everything would be fine.

Now it seems that there is a measurable difference between these two types of person. The two groups are referred to as "lark chronotype" and "owl chronotype". "Chronotype" literally means "time type". Let's just call them larks and owls.

It's not just that the waking and sleeping times are different between larks and owls. It's also that the peak wakefulness and peak sleepy times during the day are different.

Larks have peak wakefulness around midday and function and even feel happier between around 9 a.m. and 4 p.m. They are able to wake easily early in the morning and often choose to do so if they have a lot on.

Owls tend to wake later and find it very difficult to be alert in the first part of the morning. They also find it harder to go to sleep until much later at night (which obviously has an effect on their hours of sleep, as they still usually have to get up early). They do their best work and feel better and happier in the evening and late at night.

It's not clear what proportion of people are larks or owls, and you'll read wildly different estimates. This is largely because it depends what questions you ask and how they are worded. All the surveys and studies do also suggest that many people are neither strongly owl or lark.

Whether you are an owl or a lark seems to be largely genetic, so if both your parents are one or the other you will be more likely to be the same. But it's also quite possible that we learn the habits of waking or sleeping patterns from the people around us – the people in our family or household – so our environment could be a very strong factor at least for some people.

It seems that lark/owl behaviour can change over our lifetime. Young children tend to be more lark-like, as any parent can tell you; teenagers are very often more owl-like; and many older people become more lark-like the older they get.

It's also possible that modern society pushes people towards larkness and simply the act of getting up early every morning could shift your circadian patterns so that you may behave as a lark even if you are wired to be more owl-like.

Unfortunately, society favours larks. Our working lives, including yours at school or college, usually require us to wake up early. We need our seven to eight hours (or more for adolescents, as you now know) so we need to go to sleep at around 10–11 p.m. if we have to get up at around 7 a.m. And, of course, some of you will have to get up much earlier, depending on your journey in the morning.

Society also favours larks by praising them for their alertness and ability to arrive at school or work with brains fully ready to shine. Owls may be accused of laziness and lacking energy. The working day – especially at school – favours a lark's alert hours. The owl is becoming most functional just as school is finishing!

Larks and owls may also have average differences in eating patterns, with larks tending to eat more in the morning while owls tend to eat later at night. This may help explain why more owls than larks seem to have problems with obesity. Some research suggests different personality traits, too, with larks tending towards introversion and owls towards extroversion. Daniel H Pink[7] discusses research that suggests that larks tend to be introverted, conscientious, agreeable, persistent and emotionally stable while owls tend towards being open, extrovert, impulsive and sensation-seeking. But don't regard these tendencies as strong or set in stone: they are observations and ideas and may not hold true for many people. And many people disagree.

It's not certain that these differences are entirely biological. We have a variety of daily routines and we are brought up in different families with various habits or lifestyles. So there are a whole load of psychological and individual reasons that could make someone behave more like a lark or an owl. Also, some people have had success in changing their daily routines in order to become more of a lark when they've needed to, which suggests that it's not only fixed biology that make people behave like larks or owls.

It could be useful for you to know which chronotype you tend towards. Then you can make the most of any benefits and also to try to reduce the impact of the disadvantages. For example, owls can use the evening to focus on difficult tasks (but don't work too late, please!) and can take measures to wake up more easily, such as by using daylight bulbs. Larks can focus on their difficult work and exam revision in the morning and take advantage of their chronotype by having a healthy early bedtime.

Even if our chronotypes are biological, there are still lots of things we can do to shift them slightly if we want or need to. The strategies I offer later in the book, especially for getting to sleep quickly and shifting circadian rhythms to an earlier bedtime, will all help. Even if you can't change your underlying chronotype, you can make useful changes to some routines and behaviours and change how it affects your life and health. Little changes will have noticeable effects.

QUIZ: ARE YOU A LARK OR OWL?

There are lots of quizzes for this online, including a good one from the BBC[8]. I have created this one for you. Remember, however, that every human is an individual, not just in biology but also in habits and lifestyle. So, you won't fit precisely into one box and you won't always be able to answer every question easily. You also might find you go through phases. Just because you are an owl in some situations and a lark in others doesn't mean that the distinction doesn't work. Larkness and owlness, as with everything to do with human behaviour, is about averages and tendencies. We are not computers!

The number after each question is your score. You can add them up as you go – don't write in the book in case someone else wants to do it! For each question, select the ONE answer that fits you best.

A. On a school day (or college, work or home-school day), when my alarm goes off or someone wakes me in the morning:

- I am usually awake before then (1).
- I wake easily (2).
- It's not particularly easy to wake up but I manage it OK (3).
- I manage to wake up OK but I feel very sleepy for at least an hour (4).
- It is really difficult to wake up – I often fall back to sleep; I sometimes sleep through my alarm (6).

B. During the first 30–45 minutes after my alarm or wake-up call:

- I feel pretty good – wide awake and getting ready for the day (1).
- I feel neither great nor awful – I just get on with things (2).
- I feel just as sleepy as I felt when my alarm went off (3).

C. About my appetite 30–60 minutes after waking:

- I can easily eat breakfast (1).
- I can manage a drink and some cereal or toast (or similar) but not both (2).
- I find it really hard to eat anything until I've been up for longer than an hour (3).

D. If I had to do an exam, the best time for me would be:

- 8.30–10.30 a.m. (1).
- 10.30am–12.30 p.m. (2).
- After lunch and before 3.30 p.m. (3).
- After 3.30 p.m. (4).

E. At the end of the day, I usually start feeling sleepy and thinking about bed:
- Before 9.00 p.m. (1).
- 9.00–10.00 p.m. (2).
- 10.00–11.00 p.m. (3).
- 11.00–12.00 a.m. (4).
- After midnight (5).

F. The best time of day for me to do physical exercise and when I have most energy is:
- Early morning – ideally I'd exercise before school if I could (1).
- Mid-morning to lunchtime (2).
- Afternoon (3).
- Evening after school (4).

G. I feel I do my best work and have my best ideas:
- Between waking up and getting to school (0).
- During a school morning (2).
- During a school afternoon (3).
- After school (4).
- Late at night (5).

H. During holidays or at weekends, if I don't set my alarm clock in the morning:
- I almost always wake up at the same time and don't go back to sleep (1).
- I sometimes wake at the same time but I fall back to sleep for a while (2).

- I wake maybe an hour later and then usually get up (3).
- I wake much later – and staying asleep or dozing till lunchtime is quite usual for me (4).

I. **If I had to do work such as exam revision during the holiday or weekend, my best time to do this would be:**
- As soon as I wake up (0).
- Later in the morning (2).
- After lunch or sometime during the afternoon (2).
- Early evening (3).
- Late at night (5).

J. **I feel I am:**
- Definitely a lark (0).
- Probably and usually more lark than owl (2).
- Neither one nor the other (2).
- Probably and usually more owl than lark (2).
- Definitely an owl (5).

UNDERSTANDING YOUR RESULTS

Your score will be between 7 and 44. The lower your score the more you fit the lark chronotype and the higher your score the more you fit the owl chronotype. Here are some other things to consider:

- Did you find it easy to decide your answers? If you felt very certain about your lark-related, morning-alert answers, this makes it more likely that you are a lark; and vice versa.

- Would your answers vary quite a lot from month to month or between term time and holiday? If so, your larkness or owlness may not be deep-rooted in you but more to do with what's going on in your body and life. Tiredness and stress could make you sleep badly, for example, which could make it harder to wake up.

Are these waking and sleepiness patterns causing difficulty for you or are they relatively easy to manage? If you're not having a problem, no need to change anything. If you feel that your patterns of alertness or sleepiness are getting in the way of the work and social life that you need, look at some of the strategies in Chapter Eight to shift your sleeping times to something that will work better for your life.

Remember: even though chronotypes seem to have a biological basis, there are likely to be things you can do to alter your habits and behaviours at different times of day, to improve your early morning alertness if you need to.

CHAPTER THREE:

INSIDE THE SLEEPING BRAIN

This chapter gives you a fascinating insight into what your brain is doing while you're asleep. It's certainly not lounging around doing nothing! You'll find out about the different stages and cycles and what each one is for. And you'll see that your first hours of sleep are not the same as your later ones.

HOW DO SCIENTISTS LOOK INSIDE A SLEEPING BRAIN?

We would know very little of the science on the pages that follow if scientists couldn't look inside sleeping brains. So, how do they do this and what do they see?

If you are investigated for poor sleep or you ever have the chance to be part of a sleep study, this is what would happen. In a sleep laboratory, you'd be observed with various monitors to see what happens while you go through the night. The core of these tests is the electroencephalogram (EEG), which records brain activity, with wires lightly attached to your scalp. (It doesn't hurt!)

The EEG measures "brainwaves" – patterns of electrical activity between cells. It's the differences between waking and sleeping patterns, and between patterns during different stages of sleep, that scientists or doctors examine in the sleep laboratory. The EEG record or "trace" looks like a wavy line, showing up and down peaks and troughs. Researchers would either see peaks and troughs that are close together (for fast brainwaves) or

48 Zzzz

with more space between (for slow brainwaves).

Brainwaves are not like heartbeats: heartbeats are mostly regular, although they speed up sometimes. Your brainwaves are quite different and usually very irregular. They change noticeably according to your mental activity and consciousness.

When you are fully awake, your brainwaves are called beta waves. They are fast and chaotic, ranging from 15 to 40 waves per second, depending on how strongly engaged you are on a task. Just before you fall asleep, as your heart rate slows, blood pressure drops and you become relaxed, your brainwaves also change. Your brainwaves are called alpha waves at this point: because your eyes are closed, your brain is receiving less information and the electrical activity slows somewhat, to around 10 waves per second. Your EEG trace will show the moment you fall into sleep, as your brainwaves change again. It will also show which stage of sleep you are in, as your brainwaves change between each stage.

You *might* also have eye movements recorded with an electrooculograph, muscle movements with an electromyograph and heart activity with an electrocardiograph (ECG).

Surprisingly, people do manage to sleep while attached to these machines! This kind of testing has now been performed on enormous numbers of people around the world, whether for research or because they are being investigated for a sleep disorder.

SLEEP STAGES AND CYCLES

Every night each of us goes through different sorts of sleep and wakefulness. Scientists talk about sleep "stages" with different depths of sleep in each. You've heard me talk about light, deep and dream sleep. Over the course of the whole night, you'll go back and forth through each of these stages several times, with each set of stages being called a cycle and with each cycle changing as you go through the night. So, your early night cycles are different from your later ones.

The main difference in sleep stages is between REM sleep and non-REM. REM stands for Rapid Eye Movement and is when almost all (some say all) our dreaming happens. Non-REM sleep – usually called NREM (pronounced "EN-REM") – falls into several stages.

You may find scientists talking about either three or four NREM stages. This is because from about 2007 they decided to combine stages 3 and 4 because there's so little difference.

So, the modern way of describing sleep stages is to talk about REM and NREM, with the NREM stages called N1, N2 and N3.

SUPER-CHARGED SLEEP FACT
THE DISCOVERY OF REM SLEEP

REM sleep was discovered in 1952 by one of the heroes of sleep science, though he was only a graduate student at the time: Eugene Aserinsky, along with his supervisor, Professor Nathaniel Kleitman, another giant of sleep science, at the University of Chicago. People had already noticed the fairly obvious fact that at certain stages during sleep people's eyelids flicker strangely, but no one had linked this with dreaming. One night Aserinsky was experimenting with recording his young son's brain activity, when the child fell asleep. (His son, who was eight at the time, reports being perfectly happy about this and there was no danger, but scientists generally wouldn't be allowed to do this now!) After a while, Aserinsky was looking at the EEG machine and assumed his son was awake, because his brain was so active. The realisation that he was fast asleep led a little later to Aserinsky's realisation that this flickering-eye stage of sleep coincided with active dreaming.

As well as stages, we also have "sleep spindles", which can only be recorded on an EEG. These are sudden bursts of strong electrical activity that only happen during sleep. They begin during the second stage of light sleep and continue through deep sleep, when they happen more than any other time. You'll learn a bit about their role on page 58.

Now, I'll show you what your brain and body are doing in each stage. After that, I'll talk about the benefits of each stage.

SUPER-CHARGED SLEEP QUESTION
SHOULD I WEAR A SLEEP TRACKER?

A sleep tracker can only measure heart rate and movement, not brainwaves. Therefore, you'll only see "light" and "deep" and "REM" (as well as "awake") and it can't tell what stage of light or deep sleep you're in. But while a sleep tracker can't be as reliable as a sleep laboratory, it can often give you a fairly interesting record of the amount of time you spend asleep and awake, as well as a guide as to whether you were in light, deep or dreaming sleep.

Sleep trackers don't really help you sleep but they can be useful for spotting patterns in your good or bad nights. And they can be reassuring when they show that actually on that awful night you did in fact get quite a few hours.

On the other hand, they can make you somewhat obsessed by your sleep, which isn't always a good idea. It could make you more anxious or less anxious, depending on you and how you react to the tracker. And if it makes you more anxious, it's definitely not going to help you sleep!

If you do have a tracker, for the best accuracy it needs to be the sort worn on your body, not under the pillow.

SLEEP STAGES

Stage 1: light NREM – sometimes called N1
This is very light sleep, typically fewer than five minutes. Your body and brain become more relaxed, with your heart rate slowing and blood pressure dropping. If something wakes you in this stage, you'll wake easily and might not even feel you've been asleep.

STAGE 1

SUPER-CHARGED SLEEP FACT
WHEN YOU FEEL YOU'RE FALLING DOWN A STEP

This is called a "hypnagogic myoclonic twitch"! It apparently happens to around 70 per cent of people and it happens to some more than others. There's nothing you can do about it and no need to worry! We aren't sure why it happens but it seems to occur more often when we're exhausted. Some people believe that it dates from the time when humans may have slept in trees for safety and that it could have been a mechanism to stop us falling. (I'm not sure how effective that would be, as it might be a bit too late…)

Stage 2: light NREM – sometimes called N2
This is still light sleep but drifting deeper. Your heart rate slows further, your blood pressure and body temperature drop. Your body becomes more limp and relaxed. You might start to snore as your throat muscles relax.

Your brainwaves in Stages 1 and 2 have slowed to between three and seven waves every second, but still without a noticeable pattern. They are called theta waves and they move in all directions around the brain.

Stage 2 is also when sleep spindles start. They carry on into deep sleep.

Typically, you'll spend 40–60 per cent of the night in Stage 1 and 2 light NREM sleep, though this (as with all timings) varies from night to night and at different stages of life.

Stage 3: deep NREM – sometimes called N3

You're now entering deep sleep. If anyone tries to wake you, they won't find it easy and you'll feel groggy and confused if they manage it. Your brainwaves have slowed further and become more regular. Your muscles are very relaxed and your heart rate is at its slowest. As you progress into this stage, it becomes even harder to wake up and even more unpleasant if you do.

It's in this deep NREM sleep that sleepwalking and sleep-talking tend to happen, as well as something less common but very unpleasant called "night terrors" (see page 103).

The slow brainwaves of deep NREM sleep are called delta waves and have only one or two waves every second. They move in one direction, from the front of your brain to the back, rather like a brush sweeping gently in one direction.

Typically, we spend around 20 per cent of the night in deep NREM sleep, with younger people having more of this stage than adults and elderly people having the least.

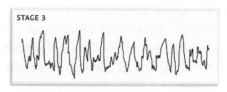

REM SLEEP

In REM sleep, brainwaves are very similar to when we are awake: fast and chaotic. A researcher looking only at your EEG trace would probably not be able to tell if you were awake or in REM sleep. Yet what's happening inside your brain and body is very different.

If you had an fMRI scan, instead of an EEG trace, scientists would see very different activity compared to when you're awake. Several areas of the brain would suddenly become active:

a.   Visuo-spatial centres – areas which enable us to process complex visual information.

b.   Motor cortex – this area operates our movements when we're awake, but, as you'll discover in the following pages, our voluntary muscles are paralysed during REM sleep.

c.   Hippocampus and nearby areas – which allow us to learn new things, including "autobiographical" memories (things about ourselves).

d.   The emotional centres, including the amygdalae – these are responsible for fight/flight/freeze and triggering primary emotions such as fear, horror and desire, as well as the stress response.

At the same time, the areas of the frontal cortex most associated with control and reason become much less active. Remember that REM sleep is when you dream; this will happen several times a night, usually after you've been in deep NREM sleep and generally more often during the second half of the night than the first. So this fits our experience of dreaming as usually bizarrely illogical. Often when you're dreaming, what's happening feels absolutely sensible but when you wake up and try to explain it you see how reality and common sense were absent.

Additionally – and fascinatingly – while you're in REM sleep, your brain's stress response is quite different from when you're awake. In REM sleep, you may have physical signs of stress, such as raised heart rate and sweating, but your brain shuts down production of noradrenaline, the brain equivalent of adrenaline. See pages 64 and 71 for a suggestion as to why REM sleep could therefore be important for mental health.

If someone looked at your closed eyes, they'd know you were in REM sleep, because your eyelids would be flickering; you might also be twitching (you'll notice sleeping dogs or cats do this, too). But your arms and legs and other muscles involved in voluntary movement are paralysed, so you won't act out your dreams. The "involuntary" muscles of your heart and lungs, and everything else you need to stay alive, aren't paralysed so don't worry! Not only are your voluntary muscles paralysed, they have absolutely no power at all. If someone lifted your arm (assuming this didn't wake you) it would be entirely floppy.

All your true dreaming will happen during this stage. By true dreaming I mean those often strange, rich, story-like experiences that we call dreams. We can also have brief, simple thoughts or experiences in other stages. For example, you might wake from NREM sleep with an idea or feeling that you had imagined something, but it will be very brief, and also very ordinary.

You dream every night, several times. You will usually only be aware of this if you wake directly from REM sleep. If you are woken right in the middle of a dream, you'll often remember extraordinary details of it.

Dreaming is so fascinating that I've included a whole chapter on it: Chapter Seven.

Healthy adult humans typically spend around 20–25 per cent of the night in REM sleep. As always, there's variation, including with age: children dream the most and elderly adults the least, for example. You'll see detail about teenagers and dreaming from page 71. Mental health can also make a difference and I'll talk about this a bit more on page 107.

It is also normal to spend some time awake between cycles. You may or may not notice these awakenings, depending on how long they are and whether you get up to go to the bathroom, for example. If you are worrying about something, it's very normal to find it harder to get back to sleep after some of these awakenings, so you're likely to remember them more.

SLEEP CYCLES

Every night, depending on how long you sleep, you'll go through these stages three to five times, in cycles of roughly every 90 minutes. But each cycle is not the same. The pattern of these stages and how long they take is called "sleep architecture". Sleep architecture is different for different age groups.

Teenagers, especially younger ones, will tend to have more REM sleep than adults but for both you and me most REM sleep will be in the later cycles and most of our deep sleep will be in the early cycles. This means that if you (or I) don't sleep at least seven to eight hours, we'll lose a greater proportion of REM sleep, as well as quite a lot of light sleep (which is spaced out more evenly through the night).

Strangely, researchers have found that if you don't go to bed until the early hours of the morning (as opposed to simply going to bed somewhat later than you should) this messes up your sleep patterns and you won't start with a normal early-night pattern of rich deep sleep. So you will lose more of that deep NREM sleep and go straight into the lighter and more

REM-filled stages you'd normally get in the later hours of sleep. This is likely to be because your circadian rhythm makes your brain believe it's going to be time to get up soon, even though you haven't had many hours of sleep.

Every stage of sleep is important and they work intricately and naturally together. I'll say more about the benefits of each stage now.

SUPER-CHARGED SLEEP FACT
SNORING

Whether you snore or not tends to depend on the shape of your throat and nasal passages and everyone is a bit different. On average, men snore more than women; adults snore more than children; and being overweight can increase snoring. And if you have a cold, you may snore because your nasal passages are blocked or inflamed.

Snoring does not lead to a good night's sleep (and not only for the people you share a room with!). Anyone who snores a lot should see a doctor. See page 102 for more on this.

HOW IS EACH SLEEP STAGE IMPORTANT?

The modern ability to scan healthy brains and see what they are doing at any given point, added to many years of research into hundreds of thousands of people of all ages worldwide, has given us a huge amount of insight into what's happening in our brains at any stage of sleep.

But we certainly don't know everything. What I'm going to tell you is based on what we believe we know so far.

THE ROLE OF SLEEP SPINDLES

Remember that sleep spindles begin in Stage 2 NREM sleep but continue throughout deep NREM sleep, too. Sleep spindles seem to have at least two roles that we know about so far: they help us stay asleep by blocking out external noises and sensations; and they seem to have a role in choosing which memories to keep and which to discard. They may also have a role in processing unpleasant memories.

THE ROLE OF LIGHT NREM SLEEP

- **Learning a physical activity** – Think of things like learning a musical instrument, a gymnastics movement, successfully aiming a ball into a basketball net, practising dribbling a ball in football or hockey, learning a new dance move or routine. If you were doing one of these activities during the day, in light NREM sleep that night (Stage 2, especially, as you're in that for longer than Stage 1) your brain works to remove faulty connections between neurons and create or strengthen the correct ones.

  When rats spend time learning their way through a maze during the day, in light sleep that night their brains have been shown to be revisiting the same brain patterns, strengthening the connections formed by learning the maze the previous day[9]. Strengthening connections happens every time we perform an action and this applies during sleep as well as when we are actually doing it in waking life. (The rats also did this during REM sleep, reinforcing the belief that REM is also important for learning skills.)

- **Creativity** – During these stages, there seems to be a relaxing of our thoughts, with them becoming less logical and rational. Many people who work creatively – writers, poets, artists, musicians, designers, engineers, architects – report having wonderful ideas while drifting off to sleep or in that dozing state of falling in and out of sleep early in the morning. The theory about this is that logic can hinder creativity: you can be trying to puzzle something out – how a novel should end or how to create a particular effect in music or art – and you're trying to do it rationally. Then, as your logical brain areas relax in light sleep, that restriction vanishes and, hey presto: inspiration! You just have to keep a notebook by your bed to capture the brilliant ideas.

SUPER-CHARGED SLEEP FACT
SALVADOR DALI

The artist Salvador Dali noticed that he got wonderful creative ideas just as he was falling asleep, so he devised an ingenious method of capturing that moment. He'd lie on his bed and put a glass on the floor beside him. He'd grasp a metal spoon in his hand and hold it out to the side, above the glass. As he fell asleep, his fingers would release the spoon and the noise of it hitting the glass would wake him. Then he'd make a note of his brilliant ideas!

THE ROLE OF DEEP NREM SLEEP

Deep NREM sleep is essential to both your physical and mental state. This is when rest and restoration happen both to body and mind. Children and teenagers tend to spend longer in deep NREM sleep than older adults. And this is what your brain will naturally prioritise after you've had some nights of poor sleep or some very short nights.

● **Growth hormone and repair** – Your brain releases growth hormones during deep sleep for growth and cell repair. Obviously, these are important for natural growth during childhood and adolescence but they are also essential for repairing cells and growing new ones. The majority of cells in your body (not including your neurons) naturally die and are replaced many times during your life. Any cell that reaches the end of its natural life – or which is damaged, by sunlight, injury, illness, for example – needs to be replaced. This process slows considerably in old age but is important throughout our life.

- **Feeling rested the next day** – If you lose deep NREM sleep, you're likely to feel tired and lacking energy the next day. People who wake or are woken unusually often during the night – parents of young children, people who are very anxious about something, people going through tough times, for example – may spend much more time in light sleep and less in deep, so they lose some of this restorative stage.

- **Processing events, information and emotions from the day** – Remember I said that the delta brainwaves of deep NREM sleep go smoothly from front to back? And remember that we get more of this deep sleep at the beginning of the night compared to the end? This fits the idea that this type of sleep has a kind of "cleaning and smoothing" effect on our experiences of the day, allowing later light sleep stages to fix those memories more strongly. A bit like sweeping the dust away before polishing the floor. This could be one reason why we have several cycles of each stage, so that we get both the cleaning and consolidating stages several times.

    It's as though this stage allows your brain to reorganise itself, sweeping away mistakes and faulty connections each night and allowing new, useful connections to remain and be strengthened.

- **Processing memories into the correct brain regions –**
  Because deep NREM brainwaves traverse the whole brain
  and are longer (slower) than light NREM waves, they can
  transfer information between more distant areas. If all your
  memories stay where they begin – in your hippocampus,
  which is the starting point of most information that we
  want to remember – this area of the brain will quickly fill
  up. These bits of information need to shift to long term
  memory areas. The theory is that this is what happens in
  deep NREM sleep.

  You'll find out more about how to use this knowledge
  for learning things more easily, including exam revision, in
  Chapter Five.

THE ROLE OF REM SLEEP

- **Creativity –** sometimes, logic gets in the way of great
  ideas and logic is switched off during REM sleep, allowing
  lateral, wacky, wonderful ideas to float in. There are many
  stories of people who have had brilliant ideas or solved
  things they'd been puzzling about in a dream. The best
  known is the story of Mendeleev's dream.

SUPER-CHARGED SLEEP STORY
MENDELEEV AND THE PERIODIC TABLE

Dmitri Mendeleev was a Russian chemist with an obsession.
For many years he had believed that all the elements that
make up everything in the universe had a pattern. When I say
believed, I don't mean he occasionally wondered; I mean he
pretty much thought of nothing else. For years. He even made
a pack of cards, with each of the elements on (the ones that

were known in the 1860s) and would lay them out in every combination he could think of, trying to find a pattern.

On the night of 17 February 1869, after yet another desperate attempt and failure to solve the puzzle, Mendeleev fell asleep and had a dream. In his dream, all the elements fell into a pattern. When he woke up, he wrote it all down and realised he'd cracked it. It may be that the story has exaggerated the perfection of the solution – for example, perhaps his dream gave him the structure and idea but he then worked it all out while awake – but there's no doubt that something in his dream gave him the solution.

Remember I said that early light sleep – as we are falling into sleep – can also have this same effect of loosening our thoughts, freeing them from the logical, controlling parts of the brain. So, this creative boost that REM sleep can give us may not be special to dreaming but just a result of bypassing the rational parts of our brain.

Writers, musicians, artists, engineers, designers and more will often experience creative insights from dreams. When we're awake, we often access the logical, knowledge-based areas of our brain when we might be better flying free in our minds and doing creative "what ifs". When we are being too rational, we risk dampening down our imagination with thoughts such as "Don't be silly – that couldn't happen" or "Well, what ought to happen next is this" or "The rules say that this is what should come next". Dreams don't follow rules, so dreams can throw up brilliantly original ideas. Most of those ideas will be useless but occasionally they will be not only brilliant but also genuinely useful. Sometimes powerfully so. Ideas that you have in your sleep could even super-charge your life, as they did for Salvador Dali, Dmitri Mendeleev and many others.

SUPER-CHARGED SLEEP STORIES
MORE CREATIVE SUCCESSES

Here are other stories of someone being creatively inspired in a dream: Mary Shelley dreamt the idea and setting for her novel, *Frankenstein*; Paul McCartney dreamt the tunes of "Yesterday" and "Let It Be" and John Lennon based "#9 Dream" on a dream; Salvador Dali's iconic picture of melting clocks came (as did many of his paintings) from a dream; Stephen King's novel and film *Dreamcatcher* was strongly inspired by many dreams he had when recovering from a serious accident; and in 1845 inventor Elias Howe solved his attempt to create a sewing machine after puzzling over it for a long time and finding the solution in a violent dream.

Note that when people solve problems or have brilliant insights and ideas in dreams, these don't come randomly: they always follow really hard work and intense attempts by the person to generate such results. You will not solve a problem in your sleep unless you really want to and work hard at it. Every story of this sort involves the person really wanting to solve the problem and spending a lot of time thinking about it while awake.

- **Stress relief** – Remember that one striking thing about REM sleep is that noradrenaline, the brain's version of adrenaline, the stress chemical, is not produced during it. Your brain is having a rest from the stress of your day or your worries. This may well connect with the next two points.

- **Cardiovascular health** – All stages of sleep are important for the health of our cardiovascular system. "Cardiovascular" refers to the whole system in which blood flows around our body. One of the key aspects of cardiovascular health is blood pressure – when it's too high it puts pressure on the blood vessels and brings risk of stroke, for example.

  In REM sleep, with blood pressure falling and the stress hormone noradrenaline absent, our cardio system gets a real dose of rest from the stresses and strains of the day. Even if you're dreaming about something terrifying, your blood pressure and stress levels don't rise. That's remarkable!

- **Emotional health** – In REM sleep the emotional areas of our brain are very active, much more so than when we're awake. So are the areas responsible for autobiographical memory: processing things that have happened to ourselves. Researcher Robert Stickgold analysed[10] the waking lives and dream content of 299 individuals and made interesting observations. He found that dreams very rarely contain exact reruns of things we did that day, though elements of them will appear; but dreams very often indeed reflect the emotions and worries of the person during the day.

  If the brain is reliving the emotional experiences and feelings of the day and yet isn't experiencing noradrenaline and its associated stress effects, could this explain why REM sleep seems to have a positive effect on emotional state? Matthew Walker talks about REM sleep as therapy and he has done a great deal of research to prove this effect. He suggests that, while REM sleep helps us build memories, it also helps us forget the most painful aspects of those memories.[11]

  Another sleep expert, Rosalind Cartwright, looked at

people with clinical depression caused by very upsetting experiences. She analysed the content of their dreams and showed that those people who actually dreamt about the upsetting experiences at or around the time when the events happened were more likely to have recovered a year later.

Perhaps we don't just need to dream: we also need to dream about upsetting experiences in order to get over them? That's certainly what some researchers believe. However, this is such a difficult field to research and the topic so complicated that it's too early to draw clear conclusions other than that REM sleep – like the other stages – is very important to humans, and that our emotional health could well be one of the main beneficiaries. Don't be afraid of your bad dreams: they could be helping you.

SUPER-CHARGED SLEEP QUESTION
WHAT ABOUT BAD DREAMS AND PTSD?

If dreams – and specifically bad dreams – are important for our ability to "get over" a horrible experience, why do people with Post-Traumatic Stress Disorder (PTSD) very commonly have terrible dreams and yet don't seem to be healed by their dreams? The answer is that it seems that they do have raised noradrenaline levels during REM sleep, suggesting that by repeating the dream but also with the original stress response, they just feel stressed every time, rather than being healed and able to "get over" the horror. Experts are now looking into how to reduce the level of noradrenaline in these patients but have not yet found a way to do this safely and reliably.

- **Emotional health and teenagers** – I'm going to cover special teenage sleep patterns in the next chapter but it's worth making a point here about the importance of sleep, dreaming and teenage health. Adolescence is a time when mental illness often starts. Modern teenagers very often don't get enough sleep; sometimes it's not their fault (early school start times) and sometimes it is (screens and messaging too late at night!). But here's an important point. If you sleep too little, you don't just lose sleep: you lose a larger proportion of REM sleep than deep sleep. More REM sleep happens in the second half of the night so cutting your night short means losing more REM than deep sleep. (However, as I said on page 56, if your night is short because you stayed up till early morning, this pattern is disrupted further and you lose even more deep sleep.)

SUPER-CHARGED SLEEP FACT
HUMANS AND APES

Human sleep is very different from that of our closest relatives – chimpanzees and other big apes – in two ways. We sleep less (non-human primates sleep 10–15 hours) and we have much more REM sleep (around 20–25 per cent as opposed to the less than 10 per cent for other primates). This suggests that REM sleep brings important benefits to humans. If we ask ourselves what things humans do better or more than other animals, two things that come to mind are creativity and emotional intelligence. Perhaps our creativity and our emotions lead us to a rich REM sleep and dream world or perhaps REM sleep helps us be creative and process all those rich emotions?

Look at the list of benefits of REM sleep. Which do you think might be more important for humans than other animals?

- **Empathy and social cues** – Reading other people's emotions is incredibly important to humans, even more so than for other animals, because our interactions are so complex. REM sleep has been shown to improve our ability to do this. In research[12], people whose REM sleep was prevented or reduced behaved in a more anxious way during the days, interpreting other people as threatening when they weren't. So, REM sleep helps us bond with other people, building those relationships that are so important to us and our success in life. This function of REM sleep also seems to come into play in early adolescence, just at the time when it's most necessary. As teenagers, you have to work your way round extremely complicated social situations and adults aren't able to help you as they did when you were younger. You're more on your own and fortunately the amazing teenage brain kicks in with extra skills just when necessary.

This chapter has mostly been about the science of sleep for humans in general. But there are some very special things to say about sleep and teenage brains and lives. That's what we're going to look at next.

CHAPTER FOUR:

SLEEP AND THE AMAZING TEENAGE BRAIN

Of all the biological and psychological changes associated with adolescents, sleep changes are among the most commonly experienced. Some teenagers will find this happens quite early in adolescence and others later. Some won't find these new sleep patterns a big problem but others will. Everything affects us all differently: we're all human and follow human patterns of behaviour and development, but we're also all individual and will therefore experience everything individually.

Adolescence is often associated with difficulty waking up in the morning. At the same time, teenagers and young adults very often stay awake very late at night. Many adults then assume that the late nights are the cause of sleepy mornings. But it's not that simple, as you'll see.

Some adolescents, on the other hand, seem to need a lot of sleep and have no difficulty going to sleep at night. I've had messages or questions from young people and their parents saying that the young person goes to sleep at around 9 p.m., or earlier, sleeps through the night and still can't get up in the morning.

So, some of you will be wanting to know how you can get more sleep; others will be worried that you're getting too much. This book should reassure you on both counts.

SPECIAL TEENAGE SLEEP BIOLOGY

Teenage brain and behaviour changes in general (not just regarding sleep) begin any time from eleven years old on average, though may start a little earlier or quite a bit later. It's usual for females to reach each developmental stage on average a bit earlier than boys, though we don't know why this is. The adolescent stage of developmental change doesn't finish until well into your twenties, long after you're legally an adult.

SUPER-CHARGED SLEEP QUESTION
WHY DO I SOMETIMES FALL ASLEEP DURING THE DAY?

Yes, you might fall asleep during class or while watching TV or in the car, even though melatonin hasn't switched on yet. This is because naps are not the same as night-time sleep. You can fall asleep in all sorts of situations because you're tired or drowsy or because you're in a warm place or for all sorts of reasons to do with being more or less wakeful at different times. But you won't fall asleep for your natural, nightly long sleep unless melatonin is doing its job.

TRIPLE WHAMMY OF SLEEP CHANGES

I talk about a triple whammy of sleep changes for teenagers. First, **you need more sleep** than nine to ten year olds and than adults in their thirties to forties – on average just over nine hours compared to eight hours in those other age groups. (Remember: these figures are average ideals, not strict targets.)

In case any adult is thinking, "Excellent excuse to make my teenager go to bed early," you need to know the second part of the triple whammy: **melatonin switches on much later in teenagers** than younger children – about the same time as or even later than in adults. You know about the role of melatonin in triggering the body to prepare for sleep so you'll realise that a typical teenager is unlikely to be in that sleep-ready state until quite late at night. And we can't fall asleep unless our brain and body are ready.

You'll remember that the other thing that drives our brain to sleep is the "sleep pressure" build-up of the chemical adenosine. You'll still have that but it will often not be enough to send you to sleep without the circadian triggers that melatonin brings.

The third whammy is the cruellest part, especially on a school day and even more so if you're an owl chronotype and find it horribly hard to wake up in the morning: **in teenagers, melatonin switches off later in the morning** than it does for adults.

As I say to adults: "You know how when your alarm clock wakes you up and you feel instantly alert and ready for action? No, quite. But if you don't, spare a thought for teenagers because when they have to wake up at the same time as you, they are not finished with their natural sleep needs. Teenage circadian rhythms won't usually let them be fully awake until several hours after adults."

SUPER-CHARGED SLEEP QUESTION
WHY ARE THERE TEENAGE SLEEP DIFFERENCES?

What advantage could nature – evolution – have seen in this later sleepiness of teenagers compared to any other age group? An interesting and plausible theory is that adolescence is all about separating you from the protection and rules of your adults and becoming independent. Adults have the role of protecting their babies and small children, including putting them to bed and only going to sleep when their children are safely asleep. How can an adolescent human – or rat, monkey, cat etc. – become independent if they are always within this protective influence? So, falling asleep after their parents gives teenagers the chance to grab some independence and to bond with each other away from parental protection. (Remember not to think about our modern lives when you try to get your head around evolution: this goes back to very early humans.)

TEENAGE DREAMS AND EMOTIONAL HEALTH

You already know that REM sleep is very important for mental health. And unfortunately, mental health can be a special challenge or problem in adolescence, as you navigate the changes going on around you, pressure from all sides, issues with peer groups, as well as your hormonal and other biological developments.

And, sadly, we know that many serious mental health problems begin in adolescence, including depressive illnesses and anxiety disorders, as well as psychotic episodes or conditions such as schizophrenia. These things are found more rarely in younger children. Scientists believe that sleep is connected to our mental state in both directions: that poor sleep can contribute to mental illness and mental illness can lead to poor sleep. And some therapists are keen to use sleep education as a way to improve certain mental illnesses.

We also know that dreams help us process upsetting emotions and trauma properly so that they lose their negative hold on us. So, you need your dreaming. But you don't need lots and lots of dreams – it's not the quantity that counts. In fact, REM sleep naturally reduces significantly during teenage years.

We need the correct balance of light, deep and dream sleep for our age. If we give ourselves the appropriate sleep opportunity and we do sensible things during the day and evening – following all the strategies and advice in Chapter Eight – our brains will do this for us. It's not necessary or helpful to try to get more of a particular sort of sleep. And certainly don't worry if you don't seem to dream

much: you can't tell whether you are or not, unless you wake
during a dream, remember.

Focus on getting *enough* sleep rather than worrying what
sort of sleep it is.

SPECIAL TEENAGE LIFESTYLE FACTORS

As well as specific adolescent sleep biology, there are aspects
of a typical teenage life that can often make sleep a problem,
either by preventing you falling and staying asleep easily or
by cutting your sleep time short, or both. This is most true in
those cultures that we might describe as tech-rich and high-
pressure, including the US and Canada, the UK and some other
parts of Europe, Australia and many Asian countries. Our online
lives may bring us great benefits but they also expose us to a
load of pressures on our sleep. This will apply to any age group
– no one is immune by virtue of age – but there are some
aspects of adolescence that may make you more vulnerable.
And there's so much pressure to succeed nowadays, leading to
overwork and anxiety in some people, young and older.

Here are some factors that affect sleep and may affect you
more than other age groups.

TEENAGE WORRY LOOPS AND ANXIETY

One of the most common reasons for any of us not being
able to get to sleep is what we sometimes call a worry loop.
Many of you will have experienced this and I certainly have.
This is when a thought or worry – it may be big or small but
it will always seem much bigger at night than during the day
– just goes round and round in our mind, growing bigger and

becoming more annoying or upsetting. Our heart rate rises and we just can't get into the relaxed state necessary for sleep.

As I say, anyone can experience this but I'd argue that teenagers can be the world leaders when it comes to worry. This doesn't mean that all teenagers worry more than all people of other ages – it's an average. And it makes sense psychologically: you have a lot to worry about and not so much life experience to help you through. Younger children also don't have life experience but they more often have adults doing everything for them, so they have less to worry about. Also, when a young child has a worry, it's easier for an adult to smooth that worry away with reassuring words or distraction. Adults also have things to worry about – often huge concerns that you may not have – but they have life experience and also established support networks to help them. Adults should be better at directing their thoughts away from the worry – although, believe me, it's not always easy and sometimes impossible.

When these worry loops happen, *both* the powerful processes that naturally drive us to sleep – sleep pressure and circadian rhythms – just aren't strong enough. Though fear not: eventually, you'll fall asleep.

When I get to the section on strategies, I'll give you lots of advice about stopping a worry loop from keeping you awake.

ARE YOU OVERSTIMULATED?

It's not just worries and anxiety that keep us from sleep: a stimulated brain does, too. Sometimes our brain just won't shut down, buzzing with internal conversations, firing on all cylinders, maybe going over all the emotions of the day or rerunning conversations that happened. I find that I'm much more likely to lie awake for hours *after* an event I've been wound up about than before it. My brain is overstimulated.

Although this happens a lot to adults, there are reasons why you might experience these episodes as strongly or more strongly than adults: you have masses of opportunity for overstimulation and less life experience to help you deliberately calm your thoughts down. During your day, you are likely to have had lots of interaction and conversations with people, lots of moments when your heart was racing (with stress or excitement). For example, each time you have to answer a question or speak in front of your class or year group, each time a teacher praises or criticises you, each time someone in your peer group says something that affects you positively or negatively, each dramatic up and down of the day.

A school day offers endless opportunities for moments and experiences that stimulate your emotions and thoughts. And it can be hard to dismiss all those things once your head hits the pillow.

Caffeine also has this effect. See page 140 for more detail about this but note that it really does have a stimulating, alerting effect and that this effect lasts many hours. That coffee or tea or energy drink (please, no!) you had during the afternoon can still affect you as you're trying to sleep.

The section on sleep hygiene (page 127) includes more about how to avoid all sorts of over-stimulation in the lead up to bedtime.

YOU, SCREENS AND SOCIAL MEDIA

Worry and overstimulation may be major causes of not getting to sleep but screen use also contributes, and sometimes significantly. The least popular bit of advice I'll be giving you – but also one of the most important – is to switch off screens at least an hour and ideally two hours before bed. Even better, remove them from your bedroom in the evening if possible.

I firmly believe that adults should follow exactly the same advice, for exactly the same reasons. So, tell the adults you live with and try to create a household rule that everyone follows.

What are the problems with screens and sleep? Let's look at this in detail.

Obviously, there are many sorts of screen and many different things we might do on them. The screens that might be in our bedroom (or that we might use in the evening even if not in our bedroom) are: phones, tablets, computers/laptops, TVs, gaming consoles and ebook readers. We need to be aware of the various ways that each one might affect us. **There are two separate things a screen brings us which might impact our sleep: light and content.**

SCREENS AND THE PROBLEM WITH LIGHT

Screens can hinder sleep because of the type of light most of them emit. Some kinds of light are more like daylight than others and can make our brains think it's daytime rather than night-time. This means that our suprachiasmatic nucleus may not trigger melatonin, so our body may not switch into "ready for sleep" mode.

All light is on a spectrum – a rainbow, in fact – according to the length and strength of the energy of the particles. At the purple end is UV light, which is invisible (and harmful to our eyes). The brightest visible light is blue, although it will look bright white to our eyes. Mid-range light will look yellow. The dimmest is red, which will look red.

Daylight is at the blue, or brightest visible, part of the spectrum. It is this that our SCN reacts to, so we feel wakeful during the day and sleepy at night.

Usually, screens that are "backlit" (including phones, tablets, computers, TVs) emit this blue, daylight-like light. Screens that are "frontlit" (including most ebook readers or screens that are set to a night-time setting) emit a yellower light that makes them less of a problem.

Each light-bulb or device will produce different levels of brightness, which is measured in lumens. A dim bedside light will emit fewer lumens than a bright ceiling light. Some research suggests that all light can potentially contribute to us being awake rather than asleep but we can't avoid all light in the evening so I believe that's not even worth worrying about. The main message is: avoid too much light and especially avoid blue daylight-like light. Which most often means avoiding backlit screens such as phones, tablets, computers and TVs.

SCREENS AND THE PROBLEM WITH CONTENT

The media talk so much about the light from screens that you'd think this must be the main sleep-related problem with them. It's not. Yes, being surrounded by a lot of daylight, whether from our windows or our screens, won't help sleep. But many people seem to be able to sleep quite well whether or not they've looked at screens.

In my opinion a bigger problem is that **our screens so often bring us content that "excites" our brain.** By "excite", I don't necessarily mean in a good way. When we say our brain is excited we mean that it becomes alert and active and our thoughts start to spin. Our heart rate also rises. This can happen because we've received a message or information, whether via text, social media, email or any messaging system or online platform, that does any of the following:

- Makes us angry, upset, anxious or stressed – such as an insult, challenge, nasty comment, bad news, worrying event, horrible image.

- Makes us excited or very happy – such as a message from someone we're attracted to, or good news of any sort.
- Makes us curious and interested – such as a story that is relevant to us or that interests us in any way.

When we pick up or look at our device, we do so precisely because we anticipate one or more of those things. Obviously, we don't want the first one but we're so wired for curiosity and social interaction that we can't help looking, even if we are expecting or worrying about a nasty comment.

Think about times when during the day you had a major conversation or incident, whether positive or upsetting. How hard was it to resist checking your phone for the next instalment? Very hard for most people! Even knowing that you've got an unanswered message occupies your brain bandwidth – your attention or thinking space – and could keep you awake.

So, our screens can bring both awakening light and alerting content, either of which can damage our ability to fall asleep quickly and therefore the total amount of sleep we get.

DIFFERENT SCREENS, DIFFERENT PROBLEMS – THE DETAIL

Let's look at each type of screen in more detail. Note that if you don't find any of these things a problem for you, that's fine: carry on. But if you don't sleep as well as you'd like, managing your screen use before bed is definitely where to start.

PHONES, TABLETS AND COMPUTERS (INCLUDING LAPTOPS)

Light: These are backlit, so all emit sleep-hindering light.

However, also note:

- Some researchers say that the effects are often very small.
- The brightness setting might make a difference – if you must look at a screen after dark, use a low brightness setting (but don't strain your eyes).
- Some devices have night-time settings – it's worth trying these if you have to look at your device after dark.
- Proximity to your eyes can make a difference – screens that you hold close to your eyes (such as phones) may have more effect than computers.
- How long you use them may make a difference – a brief glance may not have a noticeable effect.
- If you read an ebook on one of these devices before you go to sleep, in my opinion the benefit of reading before sleep is greater than the negative of reading on a screen. Put the device setting to night-time and use a dim bedside light to read. Switch off notifications.

Content: Anything that allows communication of any sort or for you to read anything online has the potential to make you more alert and keep you awake. Therefore, it is very risky to your sleep even to glance at your device if there might be a message there.

TELEVISIONS

Light: TVs are backlit and therefore potentially disturb sleep patterns. The screen tends to be brightly lit. You're also likely to watch for a significant amount of time (bad), although probably not close to your face (good). Many people tend to fall asleep while watching TV in bed, but the problem is that the screen won't switch off when you fall asleep; soon afterwards, the programme or noise level could change, waking you up.

Content: People often point out that watching TV in bed can help us not think about our worries, worries which might keep us awake. This is a valid point and I'd accept it occasionally. But it's not a good habit to get into because there's too much risk of waking up later and not being able to get back to sleep. So, overall it's disruptive.

GAMING DEVICES

Light: Whatever type of screen you use for this, it's almost certain to be backlit. You're also likely to do it for a long time and may have it close to your eyes. This provides one reason why this type of screen activity is not good during the wind-down to sleep. Really one to avoid.

Content: As with anything else you might do with a computer, there's a wide range of activities, some more sleep-harming than others. You might be playing a fairly easy, repetitive, offline game. Or you might be playing in real time with other people. It might be highly mentally active, thrilling, competitive. You might be taking it seriously or not. You might be winning or not. And some games are more addictive and high-adrenaline than others. All this will make a difference to whether or not computer-gaming is likely to keep you awake or not.

Also, the same point applies as the one I made about TV: it can be so absorbing that it helps you switch off from a worry you might have. In that case, playing a game for a while wouldn't necessarily be a bad thing.

However, if what you're doing is extremely exciting, thrilling, competitive or engaging, and/or if you find it hard to stop playing after a short period of time, such as 30 minutes, then I would put this type of screen use firmly in the category of "not before bedtime".

EBOOK READERS

People read ebooks on a variety of devices, anything from a phone, tablet or computer to a special ebook reader. (If you use a phone, tablet or computer for reading an ebook, all the above possible problems apply.) But reading before bed is such a useful sleep aid (see page 148) and healthy in lots of other ways too, that I'd still say it's fine to do it. Ideally, you'd help yourself by doing two things: first, adjusting the screen brightness settings to be the best for night-time use and, second, disabling wifi and mobile signals so that you don't receive any communication at all. That way, you keep control.

There are two other things to think about with special ebook readers:

- Can you ensure the screen is not backlit or at least has a night-time setting? The first ebook readers were specifically not backlit, making them just like reading print from that point of view. But some later versions are backlit or have backlit settings.
- Can you make sure you disable wifi and mobile signals? You now know why!

Doing your best to control the brightness and the content of the devices you use can have a big effect on how ready your brain is for sleep. This quiz will help you see how wired or relaxed your brain is before bedtime.

QUIZ: ARE YOU RELAXED OR WIRED AT NIGHT?

Select 0–3 according to how strongly each statement applies to you: 0 = not at all; 1 = sometimes or slightly; 2 = often or quite strongly; 3 = very strongly.

1. I often consume some coffee, tea or dark chocolate after 6 p.m.

2. I often do strenuous exercise (involving getting out of breath or sweaty) after 5 p.m.

3. I have some big worries at the moment.

4. When I get into bed, I usually do something on a screen or electronic device.

5. When I'm in bed, I check my messages at least once.

6. I don't read a book in bed.

7. I often finish off my work late in the evening, even sometimes in bed.

8. I don't have time to relax – that's for holidays or after exams have finished.

9. I often worry that I have too much to do and I'll never get it done.

10. I keep my schoolwork open on my desk so it's always ready for me.

HOW TO INTERPRET YOUR SCORE

A score of 10 or below suggests that most of the time you are fairly or very relaxed, but it's still worth looking at any statements where you scored at least 1 and seeing whether you could relax even more in the hours leading up to bed.

A score of 11–20 suggests a moderate to high amount of stress or behaviour that could be preventing you from getting to sleep quickly and sleeping soundly.

A score higher than 20 strongly suggests that there are some behaviours and ways of thinking that are harming your sleep. Fortunately, Chapter Eight has masses of ways to break those habits!

CHAPTER FIVE:
SLEEP FOR LEARNING AND EXAMS

So far, I've focused on the biology of sleep and how it affects our health and mental and physical well-being. But it also affects learning in some fascinating ways. This chapter will show you some detail about that so you can take steps to boost how your brain takes in information, processes it properly and then allows you to recall it when you need it: for example when a teacher asks you a question, you want to perform at your best level in sport or music, or you have an exam.

As teenagers, your lives are dominated by school and, often, exams. You have a load of other things that are very important to you – friendships and groups, romance and sexual feelings, your ambitions, your fears, home situation, life in general – but schoolwork and exams are likely to dominate. You'll be under pressure from teachers, parents, the media and yourselves.

I'll be honest: all the science points to sleep being an important factor in helping you learn, understand, revise, recall and then perform at your best in test conditions. But knowing how important sleep is can itself create a state of anxiety which makes it harder for you to sleep. Worrying about the need to sleep is a sure-fire way to make sleep elusive.

But there are two very positive pieces of news:

1. Understanding and believing in the importance of sleep will help you prioritise sleep. Then the strategies in Chapter Eight will help you make it happen. Trust me: there is no need to panic about sleep. On an exam day, adrenaline will carry you through. Let's just concentrate on putting sleep right at the

top of the priority list when it comes to exams and serious schoolwork.

2. Sleep is not the only way to boost your learning. There are other aspects of well-being which also help and which you can also have control over: nutrition, relaxation, social activities and exercise. So, when sleep eludes you, give extra time to the other things.

SUPER-CHARGED SLEEP FACT
DECLARATIVE AND PROCEDURAL MEMORY

There are various ways scientists use to describe different types of memory. Declarative (also called explicit) memory is "knowing what", involving facts, figures, events, words. Procedural (also called implicit) memory is "knowing how", involving routines and actions, physical skills, anything from how to clean your teeth to how to dance a particular routine or play the piano.

LEARNING WHILE ASLEEP
CAN WE LEARN IN OUR SLEEP?

Wouldn't it be wonderful if you could play a recording of all your exam revision notes to yourself while you were asleep? I'm afraid it would not make you any more likely to know the information the next day or when you come to an exam.

Many people over the centuries have tried this and researched whether it works. For a long time, the research seemed to give positive results. In 1942, for example, Professor Lawrence LeShan did an experiment during a summer school in which he tried to cure a group of boys of a nail-biting habit by playing anti-nail-biting messages to them while they were asleep. He recorded that 40 per cent of the group that heard the messages had stopped nail-biting, compared to none in a group who didn't hear the messages.

Other such experiments have been conducted, with similarly positive results. Governments have been interested in the idea of teaching people in their sleep, as being able to do so would be extremely useful, whether for positive or sinister reasons. Think of the possibility of brainwashing people to believe certain ideas!

Trouble is, how do we know that the subjects were really asleep in these studies? After all, we know that people wake up often during the night – perhaps they were hearing the messages during those awake or dozing periods? You might think it doesn't matter whether you're learning when awake or asleep as long as you're learning, but there's another more important problem: if you play a recording during the night, there's a high risk of having less deep sleep and much more awake time, because the voice might wake you up. Yes, you might learn something, but what you really need is good sleep! Only with EEG machines in a sleep laboratory can you be certain a person is properly asleep. In 1956, William Emmons and Charles Simon conducted what is now a very famous study – which has been repeated, with the same result – showing that learning during actual sleep was impossible or very unlikely.

There is no reliable evidence that we can learn any new information in our sleep. In fact, the evidence is that we can't.

But sleep does help the brain learn!

So, we can't learn new things in our sleep but our sleeping brain is helping us learn by correctly processing information (declarative memory: facts, words and numbers) that we learnt during the day. The first evidence for this – which has now been repeated many times and is still regarded as strong science – came from psychologist Hermann Ebbinghaus in 1885. He had already discovered what is still called the "Forgetting Curve". This shows that when we learn something such as a series of words or facts, our memory of it weakens in a regular downward curve so each hour we forget a bit more. But Ebbinghaus then noticed something odd: that during sleep, little memory is lost, whereas during the day much more is lost.

In 1924, John Jenkins and Karl Dallenbach created a study[13] which has since been repeated many times. These studies take two groups of people and give all participants the same words to learn, testing them a certain number of hours later. But one group learns the words in the morning and is tested at the end of the day (with no sleep in between), while the other group learns in the evening and is tested the next morning, after a night's sleep. The group that has slept remember more.

Sleep also helps procedural memory (for learning sporting techniques or dance routines, for example, as well as "how to do things"). It is the lighter stages of sleep that seem to benefit procedural memory most.

Because our brain is learning all the time and because we want to learn the widest variety of things, we need enough of all sleep stages.

SUPER-CHARGED SLEEP FACT
DEEP SLEEP AND DECLARATIVE MEMORY

Deep NREM sleep is the most important stage for strengthening declarative, factual memory. It sorts, tidies and strengthens connections formed by what we learnt during the day.

As you know, you get most of this deep NREM sleep in the early stages of the night. The best way to get the required amount of this sleep stage is to start a healthy, natural winding-down time early enough so that when your head hits the pillow you can fairly quickly sink into sleep and stay there for a good few hours before you hit the early morning REM and lighter sleep stages. Chapter Eight has all the advice you need for this.

DOES SLEEP HELP US REMEMBER EVERYTHING WE LEARNT THAT DAY OR SOME THINGS MORE THAN OTHERS?

Research shows that the things you try hardest to remember during the day will be the things your sleeping brain "practises" or consolidates. This is very reassuring! It's a message for us during those times when we really struggle with something: our brain will help sort it out during sleep. The problem with struggling is that we might give up. If we give up, it means that we won't get the chance to see how much our sleeping brain can do for us.

So, struggle is good. Even failure – not managing to learn or understand something during the day – is a positive, because our sleeping brain will work on it. All we need to do is try again the next day.

The story of Mendeleev discovering the periodic table is an example. He struggled and struggled and eventually his sleeping brain worked it out (see page 61).

CAN SCIENTISTS BOOST MEMORY EVEN MORE THROUGH SLEEP?

Scientists are investigating various possible ways to boost the memory-improving abilities of sleep. One is called Transcranial Direct Current Stimulation (tDCS) and involves sending small electrical currents into people's brains during deep NREM sleep. The subjects don't feel it. (This is not the same as electroconvulsive shock therapy, which subjects certainly do feel, and which is incredibly controversial.) This research was first done in 2006 in Germany, with success in slowing the subjects' deep sleep waves even further and with memory tests showing an improvement the next day, compared to subjects who didn't have the stimulation. Scientists are looking for other methods that might help us reach deeper sleep in the hope that we might further improve our learning powers, but nothing reliable, practical or safe has yet been invented. Be very cautious if you see anything like this advertised.

The idea of enhancing our sleep so that we get even more benefits from it than we naturally do is very tempting. And scientists are actively researching ideas all the time. But there's so much already available to help us get a great sleep: all the advice that's going to come in Chapter Eight!

SUPER-CHARGED SLEEP QUESTION
A TRULY AWFUL QUESTION

This is a question I've now had twice in parent talks I've done in schools. The question was, with very slight variation: "How can I get my teenage daughter/son to learn better on less sleep?" The second one even added, "For example, is there a medicine?" The answer is that there is no healthy way to do this and therefore, in my view, no way that we should even consider. **Easily the best way to make our brains work as well as possible is to have enough food, exercise, breaks and sleep.**

THE BEST TIMES TO LEARN AND SLEEP

IS LAST-MINUTE CRAMMING A GOOD OR BAD IDEA?

Are you thinking that, if the science shows sleep aids memory, it makes sense to do revision late at night? It might make sense to do your learning in the afternoon or early evening, but not late at night because the very strong risk is that you then shorten your sleep hours. You need the full night of sleep so that your sleeping brain can do its work of both consolidating your learning and restoring your energy and well-being for the morning.

Last minute cramming at night is a bad idea, therefore, because you risk either cutting your total sleep time short by doing "just a few more pages" or making yourself feel so wired that your brain takes too long to get to sleep. Or both!

SUPER-CHARGED SLEEP QUESTION
IS IT A GOOD IDEA TO FALL ASLEEP READING THIS BOOK?

Tricky question with no clear answer! I'd say that if you're enjoying reading it and find it engaging, it would make good, relaxing bedtime reading. And the sleep you have afterward could help you retain it. But if it keeps you awake or if you expect to be tested on it, better to read it earlier in the day rather than just before sleep. But really, we don't know enough to be sure. All we do know is that we need sleep for everything, including learning, and that trying to learn things late at night can hinder sleep.

IS IT BETTER TO REVISE IN THE MORNING OR AFTERNOON/EARLY EVENING?

After studying a lot of the research, I feel it's best not to attach too much weight to the various answers to this question. The reason is that each study is extremely specific: it might test recall of names, for example, whereas the revision you're doing is unlikely to be exactly that. The methods and results are just too varied and complex to tell us anything consistent, useful and realistic.

Besides, you don't usually have a choice because the work has to be done when it has to be done: probably in the morning *and* later in the day. And your life is complicated enough without getting tangled up in precise time-tables of when you should fit different types of revision in.

The main thing to look at is whether you're the owl or lark chronotype (page 40). In other words, try to do most work in the period of day when you feel most alert.

However, even if you feel wide awake late at night, you'd be better not working at this time, as it will make it harder to sleep (and you still have to get up when your alarm tells you to). Work in the evening if you have to, but allow at least an hour and ideally nearer two to wind down before sleep, and still give yourself enough sleep opportunity.

Also, **if you do have sleepy periods during the day, don't push yourself to work through them: instead, take the first opportunity to get some fresh air and a drink of water before returning to your desk.**

I had an interesting experience just yesterday. It was after lunch and I was *really* struggling to stay awake. No way could I have done any more writing. I was just about to give up and let myself fall asleep in a comfy chair when a friend happened to phone. We had a great chat, with lots of laughter, for about ten to fifteen minutes, and after that I was absolutely wide awake and full of energy. This is testimony to the power of doing something different and *fun* to wake you up!

SUPER-CHARGED SLEEP TIP
QUICK TRICKS TO KEEP YOU AWAKE

Keep a little list of small, non-work-related tasks. When you're feeling dozy and want to wake yourself up, do one or two of the things on the list. It can be things as small as taking dirty coffee mugs downstairs (and washing them up...), writing a thank you letter or email, finding a piece of info, tidying a drawer or cupboard, writing birthday present ideas. When you've done one or two, go and get yourself a drink of water – maybe put your head outside for some fresh air – and return to your work.

IS IT BETTER TO PRACTISE A PHYSICAL SKILL IN THE MORNING OR EVENING?

Because we need light sleep for remembering physical skills and because light sleep happens more in the early hours of the morning, the advice is not to get up too early. The trouble is, this is when a lot of serious sport training happens, because people then have school or a job. If you have a well-informed coach, they should know about this and have tried to find a way round it. Sometimes, it's just not possible to avoid. But do get your coaches to consider seriously how to build sleep education into their training programme.

It's probably also best not to practise such skills too soon before sleep. This is partly because physical exercise too soon before bed is likely to make you alert and have trouble sleeping but there is also some research to suggest that sleeping about five to six hours after training is the best way to consolidate the skills you've learnt. This suggests in turn that training in the early afternoon could be the ideal.

On the other hand, physical exercise first thing in the morning is great for waking us up and making us feel good all day. Just not too early!

DOES NAPPING HELP LEARNING?

It can! Very many studies have shown that napping after learning brings benefits to learning facts and figures as well as physical skills. You need to sleep long enough but not too long, though, and there is conflicting evidence on this. You'll often read that up to twenty minutes is the ideal time but other studies show a benefit from a shorter time than that.

The National Institute for Mental Health (in the US) did some work[14] with top researchers that concluded that a daytime nap can prevent information overload (presumably by moving new information from the short-term memory areas of the hippocampus) and helps eliminate the feeling of exhaustion and poor concentration that often happens when we've been at our desks too long. (However, it's also possible that simply going for a walk, getting some fresh air, having a snack or a chat with friends could have a similar benefit.)

The idea that deep NREM sleep is most important for factual memory suggests that we'd need to nap for long enough to reach that stage (which could be about twenty minutes). But if you stay in deep sleep too long you'll wake feeling groggy. And we don't always take exactly the same amount of time to reach deep sleep, so in real life (as opposed to a sleep laboratory) it's impossible to control.

Also, it's a very bad idea to nap in the evening, as this is most likely to disturb your proper night-time sleep, which is more important. The problem with evening napping is that your body-clock might have switched on melatonin, so your brain will think you're entering your full night's sleep. Try to nap before you're exhausted: napping early is better than napping late. It's also not a good idea to sleep in lessons at school...

But, if you can manage a short nap of around twenty minutes in the early afternoon on a revision day, after revising all morning, you might notice a benefit.

Whether or not napping will actually help you learn, process and remember information or skills (and most experts seem to agree that it would), even a very short nap is likely to be good for your physical and mental health. Blood pressure drops significantly (a good thing) in the moments before you fall asleep, so even the act of lying down and relaxing your body and mind for a quick shut-eye could be a healthy, refreshing idea.

Napping is not a sign of laziness: if it's well-controlled, rather than simply happening because of real tiredness (in which case you need more sleep at night), it could be a useful way to feel well and learn well.

See page 31 for whether napping can replace or make up for lost sleep.

SUPER-CHARGED SLEEP ACTIVITY
HOW ABOUT TESTING THE NAPPING THEORY?

Next time you're revising at home, either at the weekend or during holidays or study leave, try this:

1. During a morning, find some material you'd like to learn. Record how you feel in terms of how refreshed you are, how motivated you are and how positive you feel.

2. Spend some time – I suggest 45 minutes – learning the material.

3. Then have a nap. (You don't have to have the nap immediately – you can do something else and have lunch first if you want.)

4. After your nap, test yourself on the material you learnt earlier.

How does it feel? This is only a subjective exercise, not a scientific study, of course. But it will be interesting for you to see how it feels. If you want, you could try doing the same but without the nap the next day. Experiment with different patterns of work, break, eat and nap.

SUPER-CHARGED SLEEP TIP
IF YOU'RE OFTEN SLEEPY DURING THE DAY

If you find you are very sleepy during the day and you even find yourself actually nodding off or needing to during lessons, it's likely that you're sleep-deprived. So, for you, the greatest benefit to your learning will not be from napping but from taking strong, practical steps to get more sleep at night. In any case, falling asleep during lessons generally doesn't lead to deep NREM sleep but being nudged awake by the person sitting next to you or the angry voice of a teacher!

LATER SCHOOL STARTING TIMES

I've spoken about sleep in many schools around the world over the last ten years or so and the commonest question I get from both students and parents is, "If teenagers need more sleep and aren't biologically fully awake until mid-morning, wouldn't it be better to start school later?"

The short answer is that in many ways it probably would be. A lot of research has been attempted in many countries around the world, particularly the US. When you're reading any of these reports, remember that school start times are different in different countries anyway so sometimes when someone says "We made school start times later", that might mean from 7.30 to 8.00 a.m. Typically, schools in the UK start at around 9.00 a.m., the US 8.30 a.m. and some Asian countries as early as 7.30 a.m.

When scientists, schools or governments try to work out what to do about the problem of school start times, they have to ask these questions:

- If we start school later, will students actually get more sleep (rather than going to bed even later)?
- Will students notice benefits in how they feel during the day?
- Will teachers notice benefits in how the students seem to be able to concentrate and listen?
- Will measurable scores, such as exam results or SATs, show an improvement?
- What are the effects of a later school *finish*? (Less uptake of after-school activities? Less time for homework? Leaving school in the dark?)
- What are the social effects on parents who are working, on family life and on the shorter evening at home?

Experiments into later school start times often show clear improvement in the amount of time students sleep (though this is impossible to assess accurately as it has to be self-reported); students and teachers report better concentration, mood and behaviour; and test results improve. But having a shorter evening at home brings significant downsides, including less time for homework and less family time. It can be difficult to do sport training or after-school activities. And, if all the adults in the household work and leave home early, it can be a problem for students to get to school.

In order to make later school start times work, any negatives need a solution. So, as well as starting later, schools might also need to consider:

- Is it possible to do this without also finishing later?
- School, students and parents all need to work together for this common cause, with clear education about the reasons: that students need more sleep and to wake later.
- Specifically, schools need to educate families about how to fall asleep earlier.
- Could activities be before rather than after school?
- A scheme to help students whose parents work to get to school.
- Should homework levels be reduced?

A later school starting time can't just be about a later alarm clock: it has to be about making the day and night work better for teenagers. Everyone will benefit!

Later school start times on their own are not enough: we also need good sleep education. And there's some evidence that good sleep education on its own could have better results than later start times. Good sleep education is what this book is about!

CHAPTER SIX:
SLEEP PROBLEMS AND DISORDERS

Any difficulty with sleeping would be called a "sleep problem", but it would be termed a "disorder" when it becomes more difficult to deal with than a temporary or minor phase of poor sleep. So, sleep problems can range from the very common and short-term to more serious disorders which can seriously affect physical and mental health.

There are certain situations which make sleep disorders more likely – and, once the situation is removed the disorder is likely to disappear. These include:

- Times of extreme stress (for example during exams or a family problem) and distress (for example, from grief).
- Common illnesses such as colds or fevers.
- ADHD.
- Some mental illnesses such as depression.

If you are sleeping badly, it is very often a short phase, perhaps for one of the reasons above, but it can feel more upsetting and worrying than that. Human emotions and our feeling of control tend to be dominated by what's happening right now rather than the past or future and it's easy to forget that so many aspects of bodies and minds are just temporary. Try not to worry too much about a period of poor sleep: it happens to most people at some point. And many people have recurring periods like this, often coinciding with times of anxiety.

I'm not saying ignore poor sleep – far from it! The message

of this whole book is that sleep is important; that sometimes it's harder to achieve than it should be; and that there are lots of things we can do to improve our sleep.

But sometimes, for some people or at some stages of their lives, poor sleep goes beyond "just a temporary phase" and becomes a disorder. Let's look at examples of those and what you can do about them.

INSOMNIA

Insomnia literally means "not sleeping" or "no sleep", but in fact people with insomnia do sleep, just not as much or as well as they'd like and they often lie awake for a long time, which can be very distressing. It's not an illness itself but an unpleasant condition or situation which leaves you feeling unwell, exhausted and emotionally fragile as well as not being able to function at your best during the day. As I've already said, everyone has periods when they find sleep really difficult. But to be classified as insomnia it needs to be more than that.

Many people underestimate how much they slept on a bad night. You have probably had the horrible experience of taking ages to go to sleep and in the morning thinking, "I probably had two hours of sleep at most." You are almost certain to have had more and sometimes much more. Those hours of lying awake are deeply unpleasant and seem very long indeed. This may not be true insomnia but it's still unpleasant and you should take it seriously. All the advice in Chapter Eight will help.

If you are getting too little sleep because you're not going to bed early enough we wouldn't call this insomnia. You need to change your habits and you should then get the right amount of sleep.

The definition of true insomnia is when you give yourself the right opportunity and amount of time for sleep but you can't fall asleep or stay asleep long enough to get that seven to nine hours that you need. Also, you'd need to have the problem three nights a week for two to three months and you'd need to be feeling very distressed about it. Those are the conditions under which a doctor would agree that you are suffering from insomnia. (But see the SUPER-CHARGED SLEEP TIP below.)

SUPER-CHARGED SLEEP TIP
INSOMNIA AND MAJOR LIFE EVENTS

Although insomnia would need to go on for a couple of months before we would call it insomnia, a doctor would be happy to see you much earlier if you are going through a really difficult event. For example, if you are bereaved or have an awful thing going on in your life, a doctor would take action earlier. Also, if you are suffering symptoms of depression, don't wait two months before seeking help.

If you are going to bed at the right time but losing a couple of hours of this sleep opportunity for any of the following reasons, we can call this insomnia:

- Taking ages (more than an hour) to fall asleep.
- Waking once in the middle of the night and staying wide awake for more than an hour at a time.
- Waking very often and staying awake for half an hour at a time.
- Waking very early and not getting back to sleep.

The most common cause of insomnia is some kind of anxiety. This doesn't necessarily mean an actual anxiety disorder but can just be that you're having a worrying time or things in your life are triggering wakefulness. Another common cause of an inability to sleep is simply bad habits in the evening, which I'll come to when I talk about sleep hygiene. Of course, another reason is that something is waking you – other people in your house or on the street, or someone snoring. This isn't really insomnia but it has the same effect: you're not getting enough sleep.

It's very common to experience periods of insomnia at difficult times in your life. When this happens, try to reassure yourself that this is both natural and temporary: you are not destined to sleep badly for the rest of your life or even the rest of this year or month. The best thing to do is take extra care to follow all the good advice in Chapter Eight. If none of those strategies work and you are becoming very distressed by it, however, do see a doctor. A doctor can refer you for various types of counselling to change habits and reduce the thought patterns that are causing you to have difficulty sleeping.

SLEEPWALKING

Sleepwalking is technically called somnambulism and there's a lot we don't know about it, including the cause. There's some evidence of a genetic link – that sleepwalking runs in families. There's a story (which I can't be sure is true) of a whole family of sleepwalkers who woke up and found themselves all sitting round a table!

Sleepwalking seems to happen more when people are sleep deprived. Some women say that their monthly cycle affects when they are more likely to sleepwalk and some people say they're more likely to do it when under stress. Some might also sleepwalk when they have a fever and there are some medications which raise the likelihood. (If you are on any medications and you sleepwalk, mention this to your doctor in case there's a known link.) We don't know how common it is, either: estimates are that it affects anything from 1 per cent to 15 per cent of people. (Some surveys include people who have done it once and others focus on those who do it often.)

Sleepwalking is more common in children than adults. This could simply be because young people have more deep sleep than adults and sleepwalking happens only in deep sleep.

What appears to happen is that the person is trying to go from deep sleep to wakefulness but something prevents it. They remain in deep sleep but with an altered form of brain activity allowing them to move as though awake, rather than their muscles being paralysed as they normally would be during REM sleep. Sleepwalkers act as though awake: they can eat, bake, draw, get dressed, have a bath – any things they might do when awake. But they have no awareness afterwards and are not responsible for what they're doing.

Because sleepwalkers are in deep sleep, it's best not to wake them.

Somnambulism does not happen in REM/dream sleep but in deep NREM sleep. EEG records show slow "delta" brainwave activity and no waking "alpha" brainwave activity; people woken from sleepwalking do not describe any dream experience at all. So, sleepwalking is not the acting out of dreams.

People worry that sleepwalking might be dangerous. After all, if you're not aware and not in charge of your actions, might you not climb out of a window or walk onto a busy road? It is very rare for anything dangerous to happen to a sleepwalker, but it's a valid worry. It's important to discuss this with the adults in your house and see if there are steps that could be taken to keep you safe if you have a habit of sleepwalking, for example by installing appropriate window locks, removing sharp objects and keeping keys in safe places.

There is no specific cure for sleepwalking but there are

certainly things that can help. As it is more common when people are sleep deprived, improving the overall amount of sleep is a really good starting point. Being as relaxed as possible during the evening is also important. Doing everything you can to follow the principles of good sleep hygiene in Chapter Eight and making your focus to get the best sleep you can will both help reduce the likelihood of sleepwalking. Do consult a doctor if you sleepwalk more than a couple of times.

Sleep-talking is linked to sleepwalking and seems to have a similar mechanism in the brain. It's not harmful – as long as anyone who hears you understands that you're not conscious!

SNORING AND SLEEP APNEA

People joke about snoring or treat it as an irritation but it's more important than that. At best, snoring makes you (and the people near you) sleep more lightly, meaning that you can miss out on deep sleep and REM sleep; at worst it can cause sleep apnea (sometimes spelt "apnoea" and also called "obstructive sleep apnea").

Sleep apnea is when the muscles in your throat close and stop you breathing for a few seconds. It's more common in adults over 40 and particularly adults who are overweight, although there are many other reasons for it, including the shape of the jaw and throat and the size of tonsils.

Someone with apnea can end up with low oxygen levels and a very poor night's sleep, leading to poor performance the next day. Another danger is that adults with sleep apnea are more likely to be drowsy when driving the next day.

You might not know you have sleep apnea, especially if you don't share a bedroom, but if you often snore (which might wake you up), or if you often breathe through your mouth when awake, there's a chance you have this condition. If you believe or if someone else in your household notices that you often snore and sometimes gasp, or choke or breathe very irregularly in your sleep, you should suspect sleep apnea and see a doctor. Because it affects your sleep quality, it could also be affecting other aspects of your health.

A doctor may want to refer you to a sleep laboratory, which will be able to assess exactly how much of a problem this is for you. The doctor will also want to try to find out why this is happening to you. If it seems to be linked to the shape of your mouth or jaw, there are items such as a mask ("continuous positive airway pressure device" or CPAP) or dental appliance to wear at night and prevent the blocking of your airway. These take a bit of getting used to but can really work. The doctor will also see whether you are taking any medication that might be causing it, or whether you are sleeping badly for other reasons which could be sorted by changes in lifestyle or situation.

SUPER-CHARGED SLEEP TIP
ADULTS SNORING

If there's an adult in your house who snores, make sure they know that snoring can damage their health. And make sure they know that three things that increase the likelihood of snoring are smoking, alcohol in the evening and being overweight. (But remember that snoring can be caused by other things, too.)

SLEEP TERRORS OR NIGHT TERRORS

A sleep terror episode is linked to sleepwalking, in the sense that the person is in deep NREM sleep. They do not happen during dreaming, even during a nightmare. You don't remember them in the morning and the only reason you would know you've had them is if someone else tells you you were screaming or if something or someone wakes you up during one.

When someone has a sleep terror, they may scream and thrash their arms and legs around. As you know, when we are in REM sleep we are paralysed, so even in a nightmare we don't move or scream – we may think we do but that's all in the dream. However, some people do describe remembering a dream after a night terror. This could be because it wasn't a night terror but a bad dream or nightmare, which caused us to wake up and during the waking stage start acting out the fear and horror of the dream.

The same things that make sleepwalking more likely also make night terrors more likely: a family tendency, sleep deprivation, stress and certain medications. Night terrors can't harm you any more than a bad dream can. Just try to be as relaxed as possible before bedtime and your sleep is more likely to be peaceful.

SUPER-CHARGED SLEEP TIP
FOR ADULTS

If you see your child or teenager having a sleep terror, don't try to wake them. Stay calm until it's over. They are not aware of it. Read everything else in this section about sleep disorders to decide whether it's caused by something temporary, such as a fever, or longer-term poor sleeping. Take your child to see a doctor if you feel you need extra help or are concerned.

POST-TRAUMATIC STRESS DISORDER (PTSD)

This isn't itself a sleep disorder but sleep problems are a feature of it. PTSD is a mental health disorder in which a person is unable to move on from a terrible event that has happened to them. Of course, anyone who experiences something shocking, terrifying or immensely stressful may take some time to recover, but in PTSD there are specific symptoms of continued distress and the sufferer may well express the feeling that they "just can't move on or get over it". Recurring nightmares are an extremely common symptom of PTSD. Typically, the sufferer keeps revisiting the original event in their dream, to the point where they may fear going to sleep. A diagnosis of PTSD should be made by a qualified medical person, who can advise about treatments.

NARCOLEPSY – CAN'T STOP SLEEPING

This is different from tiredness caused by not having enough sleep or from simply wanting more than the typical amount of sleep for your age. Narcolepsy is a rare condition in which a person may fall asleep without warning at inappropriate times. Anyone can fall asleep at the wrong time when tired or drowsy but that does not mean they have narcolepsy, which is estimated to affect 1 in 2000 people in the UK. A narcoleptic can fall asleep mid-sentence.

The sleep architecture of narcoleptics is unusual, with the sufferer often going straight from waking into REM sleep. Sometimes, narcoleptics experience a type of sleep paralysis (see the next point) and the normal paralysis of REM sleep continues for a while into the waking state. Narcoleptics may also dream before they've even fallen asleep, known as hypnagogic hallucinations. So, not only do people with this condition feel extremely sleepy during the day, their night sleep is not normal and the lack of deep NREM sleep leaves them feeling unrested even after they've had a full night asleep.

Many people with narcolepsy also have cataplexy. (Not to be confused with catalepsy, which is a type of seizure and is not connected to either cataplexy or narcolepsy.) In this condition, the sufferer loses muscle control briefly. Some people with this condition have a particular trigger, such as laughter or sudden emotion, and they fall to the ground, while remaining conscious. This can be scary to witness, as it may look as though the person has fainted or has had a type of epileptic seizure, which this is not. The person usually recovers their muscle strength quickly. Narcolepsy is not always easy to diagnose (unless accompanied by cataplexy) as it can be confused with sleepiness caused by sleep deprivation, so do see a doctor if you suspect that you might have it. There are ways to make the condition easier to manage.

A doctor will probably ask you to complete the Epworth Sleepiness Scale[15] and will ask questions to eliminate other explanations. If they suspect narcolepsy or any specific sleep disorder, you should then be referred to a sleep expert or clinic.

SLEEP PARALYSIS

Sleep paralysis is a very unpleasant event. Unlike a sleep terror, you are aware of it throughout, whereas with a sleep terror you're fast asleep. Sleep paralysis happens as you are either going into or coming out of REM sleep and it has a dream quality to it, as though you're part of a story that's happening.

Unsurprisingly, people often confuse the two but sleep terrors are worse for the person watching – the person having the terror doesn't know, unless they are woken during it. Sleep paralysis is worse for the person experiencing it, while someone sleeping next to them doesn't know it's happening.

It happened to me once and I remember it vividly. I woke from a dream and felt that something was sitting on my chest – not just something but a truly evil creature that was intent on suffocating me. I was awake but had the impression that I couldn't breathe or move any muscle. I don't know how long it lasted – probably only a few seconds. And then, suddenly, my muscle control returned and the creature was no longer there. I never saw it, just felt and sensed it.

My daughter also had several of these during her twenties, and in each one she was aware of a terrible presence preventing her breathing. In hers, she also heard a voice speaking to her.

The best way to think of sleep paralysis is as a failure to wake properly from a dream. Your muscles are still paralysed from the dream but your brain is awake. As with bad dreams and nightmares, these are more likely to happen when you are stressed, anxious or unwell. Mine happened when I had a bad cough, which perhaps helps explain the feeling of not being able to breathe.

If it happens often, it's worth seeking help from a doctor, although sleep paralysis is not a medical problem. If these episodes seem to be linked to other anxiety, then therapies that help you relax and change your thinking patterns can be very useful. A doctor can point you in the right direction.

SLEEP AND DEPRESSION

This is not in itself a sleep disorder but sleep and depression are often linked. The term "depression" covers a wide range of illnesses. It often incorporates anxiety as well as low mood. It *can* be in reaction to difficult life events, such as bereavement, problems at school or parental break-up, in which case it's likely to be a one-off episode. Or it can be something an individual might experience periodically, without a specific outside cause. In that case, causes and triggers are more complicated and can include a genetic element, a very difficult early life, a build-up of upsetting events or a chemical imbalance, or any combination of those.

One extremely common symptom of depression and

anxiety is poor sleep. Depression is more commonly associated with waking often and early; anxiety is more often linked to difficulty in falling asleep. But that's not a strict rule: you could experience either or both.

It's now understood that poor sleep can also lead to depression, not just the other way round. This means that treating sleep problems may help improve depression, as well as treatments for depression being likely to improve sleep. This makes sense because sleeping badly lowers your resistance, strength and positivity. So, at least for someone prone to certain forms of depression, poor sleep could trigger and strengthen their illness.

There may also be other more direct ways in which poor sleep leads to depression:

1. Less early morning sleep means less REM sleep, which is necessary for processing emotions.

2. Less early night sleep means less deep NREM sleep, which is necessary for the rest and restoration aspects of sleep, so you feel less well the next day.

There are treatments for both poor sleep and depression and it makes sense to work on both. Prioritise night-time sleep by following the advice in Chapter Eight. And yes, absolutely do see a doctor. You don't have to suffer in silence.

OVERSLEEPING – SLEEPING TOO MUCH

I'm often asked about whether it's possible to sleep too much and the answer is yes. Excessive sleeping is called hypersomnia. It is somewhat different from narcolepsy, although there's an overlap as both involve the need to sleep more than most people and hypersomnia is certainly a symptom of narcolepsy; but you can have hypersomnia without having narcolepsy.

As you already know, we all differ quite widely in our sleep needs and some people just do seem naturally to need more than others. Also, I should stress that I'm not talking about long lie-ins that any of us can enjoy every now and then. I'm also not talking about the extra sleep which we usually crave and need when we are unwell, whether with a common cold, or other virus or infection that knocks us sideways for a few days or more. Here are some things to consider when deciding whether you might be oversleeping:

- If you routinely or often (when you have the chance) sleep for longer than eight to nine hours and you usually feel sleepy throughout the day even after a good night, you may have signs of hypersomnia.

- This might be a temporary phase, perhaps triggered by a minor illness that you haven't shaken off or by working too hard.

- Or it could be a phase connected with your stage of development – you may be having a growth spurt.

- The more active you are during the day, the more you may need sleep to rebuild energy levels.

- It's very important to note that hypersomnia can be a sign of depression[16] – depression can be linked to both sleeping too little and too much.

For that final reason, it is important to see a doctor if you find that you are sleeping a lot more than you think is normal for your age. A doctor will ask you a number of questions to assess whether depression might be a factor for you. A doctor will also be able to reassure you as to any other possible cause for concern. And if there's nothing health-related going on, you will probably find that this phase of sleepiness rights itself over time.

Meanwhile, you can help yourself by sticking to a healthy lifestyle in terms of exercise, diet and social activity, and both going to bed and waking up at similar times each day, with a moderate lie-in on one of the weekend days.

FATAL FAMILIAL INSOMNIA (FFI)

FFI is fortunately extremely rare. It is a type of brain disease called a prion disease. It's not something you "catch" but develops in a similar way to types of dementia. Although it's horrible to think about, I urge you not to worry about it, for three reasons: first, it's incredibly rare – so rare that we don't have accurate records for it. Second, it usually begins in middle or late age. Third, it almost always runs in families, so you would know if it was in yours. Scientists are working on treatments, as they are for the various forms of dementia.

The main and first symptom is an extreme inability to sleep, which gets worse and worse, with other symptoms such as confusion, weight loss, problems with language and thinking and other signs typical of dementia. One day, as with other forms of dementia, it's most likely that there will be ways to detect it earlier, treat it better and even cure it.

Meanwhile, don't worry about it. Your own sleepless nights are caused by annoying but much more ordinary – and temporary – factors.

CHAPTER SEVEN:
DREAMING IN DEPTH

You know the basics of dream science already but it's a topic that people of all ages are so fascinated by – including me – that I wanted to share more details with you. Dreams are often weirdly intriguing but they can also be worrying, and I want you to be both informed and reassured about how your dreams are a healthy, natural, important part of your life. I will even show you that there are things you can do to control aspects of your dream experience and certainly that there is nothing to be afraid of. Prepare to be fascinated!

DO OUR DREAMS MEAN ANYTHING?

There have been plenty of theories about this. Sigmund Freud, father of psychoanalysis who lived from 1856 to 1939, attached all sorts of specific meanings to dreams. Indeed, his most famous work is *The Interpretation of Dreams*. He believed that our dreams are hiding our unconscious fears, desires and emotions. After Freud came Carl Jung, who believed that our dreams are there to reveal our emotions rather than hide them.

SUPER-CHARGED SLEEP FACT
CHILDREN AND ANIMALS

Research suggests that children's dreams contain animals far more often than adults' dreams and the decrease of animal dreams between the age of four and eighteen is noticeable. A study in 1970 showed that animals featured in just over 60 per cent of the dreams of four year olds, as opposed to under ten per cent of the dreams of fifteen to sixteen year olds and fewer still for over eighteen year olds.

But I'd point out that animals feature in the waking lives of children more than they do for most adults, too: children will play with animal toys, watch animal-based TV programmes and read stories with animal characters. So it makes perfect sense that they'd dream about them more than adults and that animal dreams would decrease during adolescence.

We now tend to believe that if and when our dreams mean something, that meaning is quite obvious rather than obscure: dream about a plane crash and it probably means you're worried about a plane crash; you dream about being ill because you're worried about being ill. Freud would say that the things you dream about are symbolic: water represents birth, houses represent people, kings and queens might represent your parents, journeys represent death. Some people believe that there is some truth in this; others that it is far-fetched.

You'll find "dream dictionaries" or interpretations online and in books, claiming to tell you what your dreams mean. They can be fun to read but don't take them too seriously! You could, however, discuss your dreams among your friends or family and use your own common sense and intuition to work out what they might mean in relation to your own worries and preoccupations at the moment. The more you learn about human minds and emotions, the better you'll be at this.

A common idea is something called the "continuity hypothesis", which says that our dreams are generally a continuation of what happens in our daily lives. Twentieth-century psychologists Calvin Hall and Robert van de Castle meticulously analysed the contents of dreams and concluded that they might be caused by what we're doing and thinking about during our day. So, rather than dreams having hidden meanings, they simply reflect our actions and thoughts from the day. They looked at gender differences and age differences, categorising dreams based on content (animals, vehicles, situations) and emotional factors (aggression and violence, fear, positive or negative outcome). So, whatever you're thinking or worrying about or planning or looking forward to, the things that are important to you right now, are the things that will tend to feature in your dreams. Around 80 per cent of most people's dreams are about quite everyday situations – school, work, home – even though the dreams you may remember most clearly are the spectacular, weird or extraordinary ones.

But people's dreams also tend more often than not to be negative. So, although you might dream about an ordinary school situation, it's most likely to have something upsetting, stressful or worrying happening in it, something you don't like. And this is even more the case if you're going through a stressful time. We can't be sure why this is but perhaps it points towards a reason why dreaming evolved so much in humans: to help us process complex worries and difficult emotions.

If your dreams have very unpleasant content, do not worry that this means there's something wrong with you or something bad in your character: the likely explanation is that you're in a particularly stressful time and your dreams are reflecting that. Dreams help you process emotion so don't be afraid of them.

SOME POSSIBLE DREAM MEANINGS

Bearing in mind that we can't be sure why a particular dream occurs but that there may be some obvious links between them and our worries, here are some common dreams and what they might indicate, taking a common sense view. I've had all these dreams so I've included some personal viewpoints; you might have some different ideas if you have such dreams yourself.

PACKING

Have you ever had a dream about packing? Where you're trying to pack everything for a holiday or packing up the contents of your house? Often in these dreams, you don't have enough time or enough space. You're trying to pack ridiculous things and it all keeps going wrong.

You'll find that these dreams often do come before you're going on a holiday or a trip or moving house. So, fitting the continuity hypothesis, the dream probably simply signifies that this is on your mind – which you already know!

It could even be useful because it might inspire you to get on with your packing when you wake up!

TEETH FALLING OUT

I've often read that dreaming about your teeth falling out means you have an illness. But it *doesn't* mean that there's some secret underlying illness that your dreams are revealing, so put that out of your mind. It just seems that when we're not well, perhaps with a minor cold or even just feeling run down after a long period of hard work, we may get these dreams. It's one of the best feelings when you wake up from a dream like that and find all your teeth firmly in your mouth.

A version of this I've had quite often is one I call a "big teeth dream". All or some of my teeth are huge and I can't close my mouth. Then they usually start falling out (in my dream…).

BEING EXPOSED OR NAKED

People often have dreams where they're going to the bathroom but there's no proper door, or the walls are too low. Or they're on stage or in public without proper (or any) clothes on. I call these exposure dreams. We could guess that this suggests the person may well be feeling exposed in the sense of feeling uncomfortable about being looked at. Perhaps you've got a performance coming up or you're uncomfortable about your appearance? I frequently get these dreams before a new book is coming out and the more worried about the book I am the more I'll get these dreams. The rest of the time, I'm very unlikely to have one of these exposure dreams.

RUNNING WITH LEADEN FEET

Whenever I run in a dream I'm as slow as if I'm running in sand. I've had this so often that I often think I am a really slow runner in waking life. When I actually start running, I'm always quite surprised to find that I can run perfectly well in reality.

My interpretation of this dream is that I often feel frustrated because I can't get more done. I want to do everything fast and do more than I've actually got time for. If you have this dream, perhaps it reflects a feeling that you have too much schoolwork and a fear that you'll never get it done?

Interestingly, since I started running as a hobby two years ago, I haven't had this dream once. Perhaps I'm now so confident that I'm not a useless runner that this dream won't feature again?

NO ONE IS LISTENING!

This is a very common dream for me. I'm trying to shout something at a large group of people (or sometimes actually just one person) and they aren't listening. They are making so much noise that they're drowning my voice out. Then they usually start laughing at me.

Again, I think there's an easy interpretation here: my whole life is about explaining things to people and trying to make them (you!) as fascinated as I am about everything. And sometimes I do feel I can't get that message over. So in my dreams I think I am processing this frustration about my voice not being heard. If you often have a dream like this, perhaps you feel your friends or parents aren't hearing you or that you don't know how to explain how you feel?

FLYING

I am extremely disappointed that I have never once dreamt I was flying! It must be an amazing feeling. I think you could guess various reasonable explanations: the desire to be free or even the feeling that you are already free. Seemingly, I have neither of those concerns!

DIFFERENT DREAMS, DIFFERENT TIMES OF LIFE?

To support the idea that we mainly dream about what worries or fascinates or concerns us at that moment, let me tell you three dreams I used to have when I was younger but never have now:

- **Driving a car but the car has no power** – I only had this dream before I could drive. Once I passed my test, I never had it again.

- **Snakes** – As a teenager I very often dreamt about snakes. I was usually in, or had to walk across, a pit of snakes. Once I even dreamt about an iridescent greeny blue snake floating in the air in front of me. I literally never dream about snakes now. I don't exactly know why, only that it was something about that stage of my life. (You might be interested to know that Freud said snakes are associated with thinking about sex[17], which is obviously a common theme for teenagers!)

- **Hurting someone else** – This used to disturb me a lot as I thought it meant I must be a horrible person. I thought that deep down it must mean that I did want to hurt someone else. Now I don't think that's what it was about at all: I suspect it was because I felt weak, angry and powerless. Now I don't and I don't have that dream.

SUPER-CHARGED SLEEP QUESTION
DO WE ONLY DREAM IN REM SLEEP?

It depends what you call a dream. If you mean something like a story, with things happening one after the other, and an emotional power, then yes. But we can have trivial, brief thoughts or impressions during other stages of sleep, and some people might call them dreams. So, depending on how you define dreaming, you could agree with scientists who say that true dreaming only happens during REM sleep, or those who say that 80 per cent of dreaming happens in REM sleep.

CAN OUR DREAMS FORETELL THE FUTURE?

No. This is not how the world works, except in stories. I know some of you will be worrying about this, like the teenage girl who asked me about it once. She'd had an experience in which she dreamt she did something and shortly afterwards she actually did. She pointed out that in Bible stories the future is often revealed to people in dreams so maybe this was happening to her? No, this is not what was happening. A likely explanation is that either she was going to do it anyway and she'd been thinking about it, making it likely she'd dream about it. Or that dreaming about it put the idea into her head and then she did it for a whole load of other reasons. Her dream was reflecting her mental state, not controlling or predicting her future.

I asked her to think about all the times she had dreamt about something and it hadn't come true. The time it did was just a coincidence.

Think about this. You dream every night, several times. So does everyone. Billions of dreams around the world every night. Most of those dreams contain very ordinary, very common things, things that are extremely likely to happen to you at some point. Occasionally, by the law of statistics, they will happen to you the following day or soon after. You'll then think, "Wow, I dreamt about a big dog without an owner and there's a big dog without an owner." But what about all the other dreams you had that didn't come true? What about the horse jumping over a house or the car that turned into a pumpkin or the greeny blue snake that floated in front of your face? Or the time you flew? They didn't come true, did they? No, because our dreams don't change the outside world. They can't. They are just in our head, like a thought.

In other words, the laws of probability mean that sometimes something will happen that we recently dreamt about. But thousands of other things happen that we didn't dream about and for every one dream that "comes true" there are many hundreds or thousands of dreams that didn't.

LUCID DREAMING – CONTROLLING OUR DREAM WORLD

In normal dreaming, you are not aware that you're dreaming. It feels real, however strange it is. A lucid dream is when you are aware that you are dreaming and you choose either to continue or to wake yourself up. Some people can also control the dream story, once they are aware they are in it. We aren't sure how common it is but I'm sure that if you ask around among your friends you'll find some who either do it regularly or who at least have had the experience once or twice. Research[18] (based on simply asking people if they do it) varies but seems to weigh down on the idea that more than half of us have done it at least once. It's likely that many fewer do it regularly and one study[19] put that at twenty per cent lucid dreaming once a month or more. The ancient Greek scientist Aristotle, who lived over 2300 years ago, described lucid dreaming in his document called *On Dreams*, referring to times when "the sleeper perceives that he is sleeping". It's quite typical to have very brief flashes of lucid dreaming, rather than for the whole dream.

WHAT HAPPENS IN OUR BRAIN DURING LUCID DREAMING?

The studies that have been done have been very small so we need more before we can be sure what's happening, but what scientists generally believe is as follows: lucid dreaming, like normal dreaming, happens in REM sleep, so it is true dreaming. But, for reasons we don't know, there is more activity in the frontal cortex (the rational control centre of the brain) which is usually quite inactive during REM sleep. So, somehow, common sense applies in a way it doesn't in normal dreaming.

Some researchers describe the brainwave patterns of lucid dreamers as being a combination or hybrid of waking and REM brainwaves, which fits the description that dreamers give of the experience.

HOW TO GIVE YOURSELF THE CHANCE OF LUCID DREAMING

There are two things I should warn you about: first, you might find people suggesting techniques that involve setting an alarm clock to wake yourself a certain number of hours into sleep. This is a bad idea, as we all really need a good night's sleep without interruptions.

Second, the purpose of lucid dreaming is to make you feel happier about your dreams and more relaxed about going to sleep. If it's not doing this, don't do it.

Bearing these cautions in mind, here's how you could try some lucid dreaming for yourself.

Remember that our dreams tend to reflect our thoughts, fears, desires and, especially, concerns. So, the way to start priming your mind to dream lucidly tonight is to think carefully and in detail about the desire to do this, for example: "Tonight, I'm going to know I'm dreaming. I really want this to happen. It's my mind doing the dreaming so I am going to take control and be aware that I'm dreaming. I'm going to watch myself in my dream and I will be able to wake myself up at exactly the moment I want."

Then go to sleep and see what happens! It might not happen the first night or even the second. But keep telling yourself the same thing. As you know from page 112, it's the things we focus on and want most strongly that our mind fixes on during sleep, and this may be true of any stage of sleep, not just NREM stages. Even discussing lucid dreaming with friends and doing it as a joint experiment could help focus your mind on this goal.

Once you've realised you're in a dream, you're quite likely to wake up accidentally because you're in a state which is closer to waking than normal REM sleep. If you want to stay in the dream, you may need to very carefully but gently control your thoughts. However, if you do come out of your dream, you may find it easy to go back into it, as long as you do it immediately and don't disrupt yourself by getting out of bed or even turning over.

Another strategy is to keep a dream diary. By doing this you are directing your thoughts onto your sleeping state and noticing the difference between dreaming and wakefulness. You might find recurring dream themes or objects and then you can use those as items to notice that alert you to realise "I'm dreaming".

As a child and teenager, I often dreamt lucidly and I still do it very occasionally, though nowadays it's random rather than deliberate. When it happens, I can drag myself out of the dream as though pulling myself through sludge; it's not easy but it's a good feeling to know I can do it because I don't have to fear a bad dream. I'm out of practice so I can't control whether I dream lucidly or not, whereas when I was younger I could do it at will. But I suspect that all I need to do is practise to get the skill back.

HOW TO WAKE YOURSELF UP IN A LUCID DREAM

It's not always as simple as just deciding to wake up, though sometimes it is. Other tricks are:

- Try to shout "wake up".
- Try blinking rapidly.
- Pinch yourself in your dream – you won't actually be able to because your muscles are paralysed but the act of trying should drag you back to full reality.

HOW MIGHT LUCID DREAMS HELP US?

Lucid dreaming can be helpful for someone experiencing nightmares. If they can learn to become aware that they are dreaming, the knowledge that they can control the dream – or at least leave it whenever they want – is very reassuring. It would also be possible for a counsellor or similar caring person to help them create a new ending to a recurring bad dream, which they could then insert into the story to remove the nasty effect and the fear.

Some experts believe lucid dreaming can be helpful for people who have experienced trauma, including those with Post-Traumatic Stress Disorder (PTSD), allowing them to process their fears. If you have, or think you have, PTSD, you should only try lucid dreaming under advice from your doctor, therapist or counsellor.

People who do lucid dreaming a lot, especially those who can control their dreams, enjoy it as a time of creativity. It can make people feel better and more positive about going to sleep.

OTHER TRUTHS ABOUT DREAMING

WHAT'S THE DIFFERENCE BETWEEN NIGHTMARES AND BAD DREAMS?

There's no technical difference: they both happen during REM sleep. A nightmare is just a bad dream but with greater intensity or horror and it's up to you whether you call what you've experienced a bad dream or a nightmare. The more a dream is towards the "nightmare" end of the spectrum, the more likely you are to be affected by it through the following day and perhaps even longer. Repeated nightmares can have a strong effect and might make you afraid to go to sleep. Although nightmares and bad dreams aren't sleep disorders on their own, they can be associated with sleep disorders and can also be linked to mental health problems. **If bad dreams are causing you distress over more than a few weeks, it's worth seeing a doctor and discussing this alongside any other symptoms affecting your health and well-being.**

WET DREAMS

You probably know that most males from the age of puberty onwards will sometimes have a "wet dream", during which they ejaculate in their sleep. But you may not know that females have them too, with signs of female sexual arousal. Any person from the age of puberty can become sexually aroused during sleep and it is something you neither cause nor can prevent: it's "involuntary" and completely normal. It does not mean you are over-sexed or under-sexed or needing sex or anything particular at all!

Here are some facts about wet dreams:

- The medical name for wet dreams is "nocturnal emissions".
- They are more common in adolescent boys than adults.
- They are probably more common (on average) in males than females. They are certainly more noticeable in males, because of the obvious release of sperm.
- They are useful in eliminating excess sperm, so they have a healthy function.
- Some people only have them during adolescence; some adolescents have them occasionally and others often. It's the same with adults: some people hardly ever have them and some have them often.

- You can have a nocturnal emission even if you're not having a dream with sexual content.

- Wet dreams do not reduce the size of a penis or cause any other harm.

- Some people say that masturbation can prevent or reduce wet dreaming but there is no evidence to support this.

- Wet dreams are not a symptom of any illness.

- Although this is nothing to worry about, if you are concerned or embarrassed, it is fine to speak to a doctor or nurse about it.

DO BABIES DREAM?

Newborn babies spend about half their sleep time in REM sleep. By about the age of six months this has fallen to 30 per cent – still more than an adult – and they have much more total sleep too, of course, so that 30 per cent is a lot of REM time. So, we could conclude that they dream. If we believe that dogs and cats dream, it's not so hard to imagine babies dreaming.

But babies also seem to have REM sleep in the womb, at least for the last two months of their normal nine months gestation. We can't say for sure whether the same features apply as after birth but it is a reasonable guess that they do. The extra amount of REM sleep that new and unborn babies have, compared to older babies and other ages, strongly suggests that there's a benefit in terms of brain development and growth. But we don't know if unborn babies "dream" in the sense of experiencing narrative events.

Babies' dreams – before and after birth – must be quite different from ours because we can only dream about something we know or can imagine. Even imagination has to be based on a foundation of real-life things. So, just as we assume that animals dream about things they've experienced – food, humans, other animals they've met, paths through a maze, pleasure or pain – we can imagine that young babies can only dream about things they've experienced: the faces around them, humans moving about, their cuddly animals or cot toys. And, as their experience grows, so would the scope of their dreams. In the womb, what could that experience be? The mother's heartbeat? Other strange sounds from outside? A continual feeling of warmth and comfort without words?

A very young baby wouldn't be able to build stories or have narrative in their dreams. Their dream world would be full of fleeting things – and probably largely made up of faces looming at them holding rectangular objects with black screens...

Some experts argue that babies can't really dream, because of their lack of language and experience. They also point out that babies have many other things to do while they sleep, most importantly building neural pathways, so maybe their REM sleep has different purposes. (Babies are born with the same number of neurons as you or I have but with very few connections between them, and they need to build these connections at an extraordinary rate.)

Finally, if dreams serve the function of therapy and emotional processing in older humans, that need isn't there in a newborn baby – or much less so. So, it's possible that REM sleep in very young babies is performing different tasks compared to the rest of us; perhaps they don't really dream.

Try telling that to a new parent looking at a sleeping baby with eyes flickering, and twitching limbs and facial muscles forming emotional expressions! I like to think babies dream and, if so, I hope they dream of being cosy and loved and full of milk, though I suspect rectangular objects with black screens might feature!

DO ALL ANIMALS DREAM?

In all the species where sleep stages have been measured (which is pretty much all of them with the possible exception of fish and some very simple creatures), the animal experiences NREM sleep. But the only ones that seem to have REM sleep are birds and mammals.

However, scientists believe – but are not sure – that mammals which live in water (whales and dolphins, for example) don't have REM sleep. Perhaps importantly, mammals which can sleep both in the sea and on land – some seals, for example – have REM sleep when they sleep on land but have none or only a tiny amount when they sleep or snooze in the water. One possible explanation is that in REM sleep the voluntary muscles are paralysed and these creatures need to keep swimming in order to survive.

We can't be sure about this and it's possible that some other animals – whether aquatic mammals like whales and dolphins or other species altogether – do experience REM sleep but perhaps it's different in some way to the REM sleep that we already know about.

CHAPTER EIGHT:
HOW TO SLEEP EASILY

Now you know everything you need to understand why sleep is so important. You've learnt loads of facts and science. It's time for strategies: how can you get the best sleep possible? How can you relax into sleep on those distressing nights when sleep won't come? What is in your hands and what isn't? In short, let's talk about how to super-charge your sleep as much as possible so you can bathe your brain in nature's best medicine.

I'm going to show you all the general principles first. Then we'll look at tackling specific problems you might have and which most people have at least occasionally. All the advice applies equally well to adults.

SLEEP HYGIENE

The key to giving yourself the best chance of a good, long sleep involves something called "sleep hygiene". This has nothing to do with how clean you are when you go to bed! (Although having a bath or shower can also help, as you'll see.)

Sleep hygiene means understanding all the things which should or should not feature during the one to two hours before desired sleep time – as well as some things to do even earlier than that. It means controlling a whole range of actions and factors in your bedroom during the evening and until you close your eyes. It's about:

a. Eliminating all sleep negatives.
b. Adding enough sleep positives.
c. Creating a sleep-promoting space.
d. Winding down.
e. Building all the above into a routine.

Before we start, let's analyse your sleep hygiene! We need to see what lifestyle habits and behaviours you currently have. They might be perfect or your routine might be full of bad habits. The truth is probably somewhere in the middle. But even people who know a lot about sleep hygiene can have some bad habits that they might not even have noticed.

QUIZ: HOW GOOD IS YOUR SLEEP HYGIENE?

This quiz asks you to consider what you generally do that might affect your sleep. It can give clues as to what may be affecting your night-time sleep and daytime performance. And it will help you make sense of the principles and strategies I'm going to offer.

For each question, select the statement that most accurately reflects the truth for you. If the answer varies a lot, you can select more than one.

If you are or have recently been ill, for example with a fever, wait till you've recovered to take the quiz, as it's normal for sleep needs and patterns to change significantly during illness.

Try to answer these questions honestly.

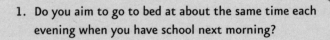

1. Do you aim to go to bed at about the same time each evening when you have school next morning?

    a. Yes, I aim for a particular time and almost always achieve it.
    b. I try but I often don't succeed.
    c. No, I don't have any kind of target and my bedtime is random.

2. Do you go to bed at around the same time when you don't have school next day?

   a. I usually or always go to bed at roughly the same time.
   b. My usual bedtime during holidays and weekends is much later.
   c. My usual bedtime during holidays and weekends is much earlier.

3. Do you have a very long lie-in at weekends (getting up 3+ hours later than weekdays)?

   a. No.
   b. I usually/often do on Saturday but not on Sunday.
   c. I usually have a long lie-in on both Saturday and Sunday.

4. Do you have a nap (or fall asleep in front of the TV) after school?

   a. No. If I was tired I would just go to bed early, not have a temporary nap.
   b. Occasionally, if I'm really tired.
   c. I quite often do this.

5. Which of these best describes your situation?

   a. I have my own bedroom and I'm not disturbed by other noise from inside or outside my household.
   b. I share a bedroom but this doesn't affect my sleep.
   c. I have my own bedroom but I'm often disturbed by noise from elsewhere.

d. I share a bedroom and I am often prevented from sleeping or I'm woken up by the other person.

6. **What is the typical atmosphere in your house in the evenings?**

    a. Pretty calm.
    b. Busy but positive.
    c. Noisy and rather unpredictable.
    d. There's often a highly stressful atmosphere.

7. **Can you see any daylight through your curtains/blinds when they are shut?**

    a. No, my room is very dark when my curtains are shut.
    b. My curtains/blinds are fairly thick but I can easily tell if it's light outside.
    c. My curtains/blinds are thin or don't fit well and my room is not very dark if it's light outside.

8. **Do you do strenuous physical exercise after about 6 p.m.? (This means any exercise that raises heart rate – running, gym, football etc.)**

    a. Never or rarely.
    b. One to three times a week.
    c. Most evenings.

9. **How often do you consume caffeine after 3 p.m.? (Caffeine is usually found in coffee, tea, cola, energy drinks and chocolate, unless "caffeine-free".)**

    a. I avoid it entirely, or almost so.

b. I do sometimes have caffeine between 3 p.m. and about 6 p.m. but not after that.

c. I have caffeine when I feel like it and that might include after 6 p.m.

10. Do you have any screens on during the 1.5 hours before turning your light out? (This includes phone, tablet, computer, TV, gaming console.)

a. I always switch everything off 1.5 or more hours before getting into bed.

b. I use some screens during this time because I find them relaxing.

c. I use some screens during this time because I need them for schoolwork.

d. I do switch them off but I often switch something on again.

e. I just keep my phone on because I use it as an alarm clock.

11. Do you read (for recreation, not work) before bed?

a. Yes, I often read for pleasure, always or usually a printed book.

b. Yes, I often read for pleasure, always or usually on an ebook reader not connected to internet.

c. Yes, I often read for pleasure, always or usually on an internet-enabled tablet or ebook reader.

d. No, I never or almost never read before sleeping.

12. Do you listen to music during the 1.5 hours before switching your light off?

a. I often listen to music and I'd choose something gentle, soft and slow.

b. I often listen to music and I'd choose anything I liked, whether fast dance music or something slower.

c. No, I never or almost never listen to music at this time.

13. Do you take regular medications for any illness or medical condition, including pain? (This does not include things you might take for a short illness.)

a. No.

b. Yes, but I only take it/them in the morning.

c. Yes, I take medication(s) in the evening.

14. Do you have a set routine of actions leading up to bedtime?

a. Yes, I'm aware I do this.

b. No, I don't.

c. I have never thought about this so I'm not sure.

HOW TO ANALYSE YOUR RESULTS

This is not a points-scoring quiz but will highlight things you are doing that can often affect sleep, even though you might not have noticed. Here is a guide to which of the following pages is relevant to each question. Once you've read the rest of my guidance, on page 145 you'll find an activity that will allow to you use this quiz to guide your new, healthy, super-charged sleep habits!

Questions 1–4 – Page 135 will show you how to create a pattern of sleep and waking, whether for term-time or holiday, that will allow you to have the healthiest amount of sleep you can. You'll see the importance of sticking to a pattern and not breaking it with a double long lie-in.

Questions 5–7 – Pages 134–138 look at the conditions you sleep in, how they can affect sleep and what you can often do about them.

Questions 8–13 – Pages 138–142 cover the things which are positive or negative influences on sleep so that you can start to see how your sleep hygiene might be improved by some simple changes. Then you will be able to try to eliminate all the negative influences and build in as many positive ones as possible.

Question 14 – Pages 142–143 are all about how and why creating an appropriate routine leading up to bedtime helps control your body clock to trigger sleep earlier, so that you can get more sleep by falling asleep more quickly. There'll be examples of how to do this.

So, sleep hygiene is about doing the right things and avoiding the wrong things in the one to two hours before it's time to sleep. Let's look at what those things are and how to put sleep hygiene into practice.

A FIVE-POINT PLAN FOR SLEEP

This is your basic blueprint for sleep. It reveals five ways you can improve your sleep hygiene and switch your brain into sleep mode.

FIRST, WORK OUT YOUR DESIRED SLEEP TIME

This is so that you know when your sleep hygiene period should start. Do this by **working out when you should be falling asleep so as to give yourself a "sleep opportunity" of**

seven to nine hours. Although you've learnt that nine hours is biologically ideal for an average teenager, don't over-focus on this, partly because everyone is a bit different and partly because it could be unrealistic. For example, if you have to get up as early as 6 a.m., aiming for nine hours means going to sleep at 9 p.m. Some of you could do this and would enjoy doing so but for most it will be unrealistic. It's not sensible to set unachievable goals.

As an example, imagine your alarm clock has to go off at 6.30 a.m. and you've decided you want to aim for eight hours. You'd want to fall asleep at 10.30 p.m. so your lights-off time would need to be 10.15 p.m. or so. Your winding-down period of sleep hygiene needs to be at least one and a half hours so would start at 8.45 p.m.

In your notebook, write down:

a. My alarm is set for:........
b. I'm aiming for approximately .... hours of sleep
c. So I want to fall asleep at around ....
d. I will turn off my light ten to twenty minutes before this, at ....
e. Therefore, I will start my winding-down period of one and a half hours at ....

SECOND, CONTROL YOUR SLEEPING SPACE

The ideal sleeping space is:

Quiet enough – Some people are lighter sleepers and more sensitive to noise than others. Also, if we are feeling stressed about sleep we are likely to be more sensitive to even small noises such as the sound of someone breathing or a clock ticking. You may not have full control over the situation but there are always things you can do to avoid being disturbed by noises.

Here are some things to think about:

- Play quiet music on a loop, set at just the right volume to distract you from other noises.

- Use ear-plugs – if you're worried about not hearing your alarm, there are a few strategies: you can ask someone to check you've woken up; you can just wear one ear-plug; you can also be reassured that you probably still will wake up, especially if you ensure that your alarm is set to continue to ring until you switch it off.

- Move your bed further from the source of noise – even a short distance can make a difference.

- If the noise is caused by someone in your house, can you do something to make them understand and try to moderate their noise?

Cool enough – Your body naturally lowers its core temperature during sleep, and if your room is too hot your body can't reach that lower temperature and you may find it harder to sleep. You don't want to be too cold but keeping your room slightly cooler than would be comfortable if you were out of bed is what to aim for.

Here are some things to think about:

- If the heating is on in your house, make sure it's turned off in your bedroom well before you get into bed.

- If it's summer and either you can't sleep with an open window (for security or outside noise, for example) or the air outside is so hot that it wouldn't help, you might try a fan. However, some people will notice dust allergies get worse and that the dry air makes their nose and throat feel dry. It's best not to run the fan all night but just to use it to cool your room before sleep.

- A wet face cloth applied to your bare skin (kept in a bowl of water by your bed) can provide instant temporary relief as air on damp skin has a cooling effect.

- Obviously, your bed clothes will make an enormous difference. In hot weather, use a cool cotton sheet instead of a duvet. Stick your feet out of the bottom!
- A cool or luke-warm (not cold) shower before bed, or running cold water onto your wrists, or placing a face-cloth in the freezer for a few minutes before putting it on your forehead are all likely to help you cool down.
- Avoid a hot drink before bed.

Dark enough – This is one of the most important things we need to trigger sleep. If your brain detects daylight (which it can do even while your eyes are closed) it will "think" it's time to be awake, not asleep. There's a lot you can do to control the darkness in your room – including choosing appropriate light-bulbs when you do need light.

Here are some things to think about:

- Ideally, use good quality (and well-fitting) blackout curtains or a blind. Any curtains can be fitted with a blackout lining, which is not usually black but a white or cream material which lets no light through. It's not expensive either and you might have someone in your family who can make simple blackout-lined curtains. A blackout roller-blind is fairly inexpensive and for most windows is simple to fit without professional help. Often you'll get a sliver of daylight appearing at the edges of a blind, depending on how it's fitted, but usually this isn't enough to spoil your sleep.
- Wear an eye-mask. This is a very cheap and effective solution. They can be a bit uncomfortable and scratchy but

it should be possible to find one that works for you. Look out for one made of soft padded material, with a Velcro fastening. You can also sew a piece of lint or felt around any bit that feels uncomfortable to you. You could even make one yourself, using felt and Velcro.

- Daylight also comes from our screens, as you saw on page 75. So, turning off your phone, tablet, computer, TV and gaming console as you wind down to sleep are all important parts of ensuring lack of daylight.

- You'll need to be able to see, so you need some electric light! Make sure you have the least amount of light you can manage while not straining your eyes. For example, turn off your main light and just have a bedside light and avoid shining it directly at yourself.

- Some electric bulbs emit warm "yellow" light, which is very different from daylight, but other bulbs emit "blue" light, which looks white to our eyes, like daylight. Make sure you do not use any daylight bulbs in the evening. See page 147 for details of different bulbs.

SUPER-CHARGED SLEEP TIP
A DAYLIGHT BULB FOR THE MORNING

While you need to avoid daylight bulbs when you're trying to get ready for sleep, waking up to a special daylight bulb will help tell your brain that it's morning and time to switch off the melatonin. You can also buy alarm clocks that switch on a daylight bulb automatically and this is helpful for lots of people, though they are not at all cheap.

Safe enough – We are wired to be alert when we don't feel safe, so we won't fall asleep if this is how we feel. This is why anxiety keeps us awake: the brain doesn't really distinguish between anxiety about something abstract and anxiety about immediate danger.

This can be hard to manage but these strategies are definitely worth trying:

- Don't have your bed too close to the door – subconsciously this can cause very natural anxiety.
- If worries about security are affecting your sleep, you could talk to an adult about getting special locks on your window, or a similar solution for your bedroom door.
- Is there something temporary going on that is making you anxious not just about sleeping but more generally? If so, could you perhaps sleep in the same room as another family member for a while?

THIRD, CONTROL YOUR SLEEP NEGATIVES AND POSITIVES

This is at the core of sleep hygiene. **We need to know all the things to avoid (sleep negatives) and things that are good to include (sleep positives) in that crucial one and a half hours before we turn our light off and close our eyes.**

Sleep positives – You don't have to do all of these but try to include as many as you can in your routine.

- **Darkness or dim light** – block sunlight, switch off screens and turn off bright lights.
- **A shower or bath** – during hot weather, a cool or slightly

warm shower is better than a hot one but in other months a hot bath can help: it can relax you and your core body temperature will drop when you get out of the bath, and this can help your body signal sleep.

- **Soft, slow music.**
- **A scent you like** – a scented candle, for example (follow safety rules). You can also get a room spray that's blended to promote sleep.
- **Lavender oil** – this can be a few drops in a bath, or in a tea-light burner, or on a pillow.
- **Smooth and straighten your bedclothes** so that you'll be comfortable.
- **Do some stretches** or a few minutes of gentle yoga.
- **A light snack if you are hungry** – good examples would be a small sandwich, cheese and apple, some hummus on oatcakes, a few nuts, a banana.
- **A milky drink or a herbal tea** – but if you find that you often wake up to go to the bathroom, make this a very small drink. (Note that although herbal tea can help, I'm not advocating the use of herbal sleeping pills. See page 169 for my argument about this.)
- **Get organised for the morning,** including putting the things you'll take to school in a pile by the door.
- **Tidy your room a bit** – at least put your clothes away.
- **Get into your sleeping clothes.**
- **Read a book** (not for work unless it's also genuine enjoyment) once you're in bed. Other good activities in bed are writing a diary (or writing anything for pleasure), doodling or doing a puzzle (not on an internet-connected screen).

Sleep negatives – Avoid these completely in the pre-bed period.

- **Daylight** – from outside and from screens.
- **Caffeine** – including coffee and tea (unless decaf or herbal/ fruit).

SUPER-CHARGED SLEEP FACT
THE TRUTH ABOUT CAFFEINE

1. Caffeine is a stimulant, sending adrenaline round the body and raising heart rate. It gives us a buzz of alertness.

2. Decaffeinated tea and coffee still contain some caffeine, just with reduced levels, so you'd do better to avoid decaf, too. Stick to drinks that are "caffeine-free".

3. Caffeine takes longer than you might think to leave the body. Everyone processes it at different speeds and some people are more sensitive than others, but the effects can last for up to eight hours. To give yourself the best chance of sleep, avoid it from lunchtime onwards.

- **Arguments** – these can be hard to avoid but you'll do yourself a big favour if you do! This is one important reason for switching screens off, especially those that may allow you to continue any of the stressful situations that began earlier in the day. Make sure your adults know that having arguments late at night isn't helpful for anyone – though, of course, sometimes adults do need to raise legitimate complaints and sometimes this is the only time to do it.
- **Screens (apart from ebook readers)** – it's not only the daylight and the stress that make our screens sleep

negatives: it's also the fact that so much of what we do on screens is likely to wake us up, whether it's watching an exciting video or TV programme full of movement and light, seeing something horrible on the news, being contacted by a friend or stranger, or doing our work, our screens are more often likely to wake us up than calm us down.

- **Physical exercise that raises your heart rate** – the common view is that you're best to avoid this for at least four and ideally six hours before sleep time.

- **A large meal** – when we fall asleep, our digestive system slows significantly so we are likely to wake in the night with an unpleasant feeling of fullness or nausea if we've eaten a lot just before bed.

- **Work** – there are two reasons for avoiding working in the lead-up to bed: first, it's likely to wake your brain up and, second, you know from page 89 that it's not the best learning opportunity. The best thing you can do for your work is to get good sleep.

- **Loud, fast music** – likely to wake you up and excite you.

- **An untidy bedroom** – I acknowledge that not everyone will experience this but many people do find being in a chaotically messy space stressful rather than relaxing. Since what we need is a relaxed state of mind for sleep to happen quickly and easily, it makes sense to avoid going to sleep in a mess. This is particularly true if your mess includes various things you need to take to school in the morning. You'll help yourself relax – and give yourself less stress next morning – if you can at least tidy the things you need for tomorrow.

- **Alcohol** – because drunk people fall asleep, some individuals might be tempted to use alcohol to aid sleep but this is a very bad mistake. Alcohol disrupts sleeping patterns significantly; drinkers usually wake in the middle of the night dehydrated and ill. Alcohol does not aid sleep. Even a small amount of alcohol raises heart rate, which lowers the restorative powers of sleep.

FOURTH, CREATE A ROUTINE – AND STICK TO IT

Once you've made your sleeping space as perfect as possible and you know all the sleep negatives and positives for your evening wind-down time, the next step is to create a routine.

This is extremely important. It has a bigger effect on ability to fall asleep than most people imagine. Remember how our circadian rhythms and melatonin timing are controlled partly by darkness and partly by other aspects of our daily routines? Well, this is where you can start to take real control of your suprachiasmatic nucleus! You can't control when darkness falls but you can control the other things your SCN notices.

There are two reasons for the effect of routines. First, a pattern, habit or routine allows the brain to use less energy on that activity and us to pay less attention. New things wake us up and familiar things make us relax. And you don't want to be alert when you're preparing for sleep.

Second, and more importantly, a simple routine can quickly become such a strong habit that the very start of the routine triggers the brain to do the thing it expects: prepare for sleep. In other words, if for a few days in a row you do A, E, C, D and B in the same order at the same time and then switch your light off and close your eyes, the brain will recognise "A" as being the beginning of this routine that ends in sleep.

In this way, you can shift the time your melatonin switches

on. You can change your body clock to start feeling sleepy at 9.30 p.m. instead of 10 p.m., for example.

HOW TO CREATE THIS ROUTINE

It has to be your routine, chosen by you, but here are some important rules:

- You should select a few (I suggest four to six) things from the "sleep positives" list on page 138.
- The first one must be creating darkness, including switching off screens.
- You can add other things you think would be restful and calming – such as giving yourself a foot or hand massage, writing a couple of sentences of a sleep diary, writing three good things about the day or three things you hope for tomorrow.
- Put them in an order that makes sense – e.g. the snack has to come before doing your teeth! Write them down.
- You already decided on page 134 when this winding-down routine needs to start. Now just do it!

SUPER-CHARGED SLEEP TIP
SET A REMINDER

Set an alert to tell you when to start your winding-down routine. Make the noise a gentle one and something that's different from other alerts.

FIFTH AND FINALLY, DO THE RIGHT THINGS WHEN YOU'RE IN BED!

You've done everything right during the evening and finished your routine by getting into bed. You might be reading for a while or listening to music or writing your diary. What then? You know roughly what time you need to turn your light off but don't be too rigid about this. It is not a competition to fall asleep at a precise time. This is about creating a sleepy mode in your brain so that sleep will come easily, not too long after you turn your light off. Once you are in bed, here are a few tips:

- Don't think about sleep. You won't get to sleep by trying to go to sleep.
- Don't look at your clock after you've turned your light out. It won't help.
- Focus on loosening your muscles and sinking into the bed. Soften each set of muscles from your toes up to your head and face.
- Slow your breathing, with your muscles softening even more with each out breath.
- Let your mind drift – don't worry where your thoughts go at first.
- Try not to think of any of those things too firmly or rigidly – relax!

There's every chance that within a short space of time you'll fall asleep. But if your mind is racing and sleep feels nowhere near after what feels like about twenty minutes, it's time for some different strategies. I'll talk about these in Chapter Nine.

PRE-SLEEP CHECKLIST

There was a lot of information in the last few pages so here's a checklist for you to make sure you've done everything you possibly can to prepare yourself and your sleeping space for bed. There's a template online for you to print so you can use this for a few days. See www.nicolamorgan.com and find the page for this book.

- I've done everything I can to ensure I won't be woken by noise.
- I have ear-plugs if necessary.
- The other people in my house know I'm going to sleep.
- My room is not too hot or too cold.
- My curtains or blinds are closed.
- Bright lights are off.
- All my screens are off.
- If I am using my phone as a clock, it's on silent or sleep mode.
- My phone/clock is positioned where I won't see it.
- I feel safe in my room.
- I have a drink of water beside my bed.
- I've made sure I'm not hungry.
- I've put any work away tidily and out of sight.
- I've got my things ready for tomorrow morning.
- I've done my pre-bed routine.
- I've done my best to wind-down and feel relaxed.
- I've washed and done my teeth and got into my nightwear.
- I've said good night.
- I'm in bed!

SUPER-CHARGED SLEEP QUESTIONS

CAN TECHNOLOGY AND APPS HELP WITH SLEEP?

As you know, looking at our phones or other electronic devices is generally not a good idea in relation to wanting to get to sleep quickly. But are there some ways that tech can help us, if we're careful?

CLOCK OR "BEDTIME" FEATURES ON SMARTPHONES

Despite the strong advice to switch your phone off and ideally keep it out of your bedroom at night, if you take certain steps and can trust yourself to obey them, certain clock features or apps installed on many smartphones may help your sleep. If you do use any such digital features, make sure of the following:

- The app automatically turns off all notifications and calls from the moment of setting the sleep time.
- It automatically sets the screen to a dim setting during the hours of intended sleep.

SLEEP APPS?

I won't name any, as they change and improve all the time, but you'll easily be able to find what's available now for your device.

Some of them involve listening to relaxing stories. Personally, I found all the stories I've heard very boring. Maybe they are supposed to bore you to sleep? I find that the opposite happens because a) the boredom means I'm not engaged in the story and b) I become intensely irritated by the quality of the writing. But everyone's different and perhaps you can find some stories that work for you.

Others involve relaxing music, "white noise" or sounds such as whale song or rain falling or the wind. Make sure:

- You can set them to play for a particular time.
- Your device is set at the lowest volume you can manage.
- Your device is set to silence all calls and alerts.

DO DIFFERENT LIGHT-BULBS MAKE A DIFFERENCE TO SLEEP?

Indeed. It's not as simple as bright or dim or even daylight versus light-bulbs. One very easy change you could make to your bedroom concerns light-bulbs. The cleverest thing you can do, if you're able to, is to **have two different lights, one for use during daytime when you want to be alert and a different one for the evening while you're getting ready for bed.** This isn't as difficult (or expensive) as it might sound, as you just need to make sure that at least one light is for each, so that you can make the choice. They can both be ordinary lamps but just have a different light-bulb.

Light to make you feel wakeful:

- Daylight.
- Halogen bulbs.
- LED bulbs.
- Fluorescent bulbs – spiral, low-energy bulbs called Compact Fluorescent Bulbs or CFBs.
- Electronic devices, especially when close to you.

Traditional "incandescent" bulbs can work for either sleepiness or wakefulness – when these are bright (100W) they are best for daytime wakefulness; when dimmer (40 or 60W, and especially when not pure white) they are better for evening sleepiness.

Light to make you feel sleepy:

- Red or pink light.
- The dimmest incandescent bulbs, e.g. 40W or 60W.

You can also buy smart bulbs, which change colour depending on the time of day, or special night-time bulbs. They are pricey but worth considering. Discuss with the adults in your house to see if one might be worth trying.

WHAT ABOUT WAKE-UP LIGHTS?

These are not cheap though they're coming down in price, as most new technology does, and there's a variety on the market. These devices all wake you up using light that mimics daylight, and usually with your choice of sound or radio station, but different models have extra features such as sleep trackers and various features to help you fall asleep, too. They all centre round the science of different light wavelengths and are often sold to help treat a type of seasonal depression called SAD (Seasonal Affective Disorder). Many people find these very helpful.

WHY DOES READING HELP US SLEEP?

Do you find that reading sometimes makes you fall asleep too quickly? There you are, snuggling down in bed ready to switch off your mind, you open your book, find where you left off, and a few seconds later your eyes are closing and you're too sleepy to read. This is obviously great if sleep is your main aim but not so much if you really want to get into the book. But with this book, sleep is my main aim so you have my permission to fall asleep reading it!

Why does this happen? I've been interested in the science and psychology of reading for a long time and **I think there**

are three main reasons why reading helps very many people fall asleep quickly.

First, reading any book we're interested in engages our attention and doesn't allow us to keep fretting about our worries. Worries take a lot of brain bandwidth; reading takes a lot of brain bandwidth; so an exciting book takes over and stops us worrying about other things. We have to focus on the book.

Second, and connected, reading is very often a relaxing activity. How this works depends on the book but whether it lowers or raises our heart rate, both can have a relaxing effect. If our heart rate lowers (because, perhaps, we stop worrying about our real-life stresses) that's obviously relaxing; if our heart rate rises through the strong emotions of the book – a bit like a scary fairground ride – we can feel exhilarated, excited and uplifted by this emotion that isn't part of our real life. Scary fairground rides are stress-busters for many people, in the same way as thrilling books can be.

Third, it's the brain's love of habit. Many people have lives in which the book-before-sleep habit is incredibly deeply ingrained, since early childhood. As a small child you may have had the following routine: bedtime wind-down (perhaps including a bath or wash, game, getting into pyjamas) followed by being tucked up in bed, read a story and then goodnight, followed by sleep. This routine will have changed only slightly, with the main difference being that you'll now read your own story. So that habit – wind-down routine, bed, book, light off, sleep – is deeply ingrained, even if you had gaps when it didn't happen. As a teenager or adult, you do your wind-down routine, get in to bed, open your book and zzzzzz.

Oh, and reading also brings a mass of other benefits: to mental health, knowledge, vocabulary, empathy, creativity, stress relief. And it opens your mind to new, fascinating ideas.

However, we sometimes find that a book is so engaging that we can't stop reading it. In this case, we should be strong and put it down after what feels like a sensible number of pages.

DOES EXERCISE AFFECT SLEEP?

Yes. I've mentioned exercise several times in passing so it's time to give a bit more detail. There's a difference between strenuous exercise and gentle exercise. "Strenuous" would be anything that raises the heart rate, such as going for a run or playing football or basketball. Gentle would be something that doesn't, such as a leisurely walk or light stretching or yoga. Some exercise could count as either, depending on how fast you do it, such as swimming or walking.

There are some simple guidelines about this:

1. Strenuous exercise during the morning or early afternoon seems to help many people sleep better that night. Whether this is psychological or physical is unclear but it is true for many.

2. Strenuous exercise in the evening seems to hinder sleep for many. The closer to bedtime this is, the more likely it is to have a negative effect.

3. Gentle exercise near bedtime can help many people wind down and feel calmer. It can also be a useful part of the "routine".

Exercise strengthens your body, reading strengthens your mind; sleep does both and both help you sleep. What a team!

DOES DIET AFFECT SLEEP?

Yes, there are certain things that will help or hinder sleep.

FOOD IN THE EVENING

In the evening, certain foods can have a direct positive or negative effect on sleep. Not everyone will be equally affected but if you want to improve your sleep, think about what you eat in the evening.

Digestion slows right down during sleep so any food should be small and light. You don't want to go to bed full, or you're likely to wake up feeling nauseous.

Some people suffer from indigestion at night, including a condition called acid reflux (or oesophageal reflux) where a little bit of the natural acid in our stomach rises up the oesophagus (food pipe), causing pain and discomfort in the chest. This pain is sometimes called heartburn and is almost always made worse by eating the foods mentioned below.

NEGATIVE FOR SLEEP:

- Caffeine – coffee, tea, cola, energy drinks, dark chocolate (including as a cocoa drink, but a milky chocolate drink is fine).
- Too much food of any sort.
- Rich food – e.g. food with high fat content.
- Spicy food – e.g. curries, especially if you're not used to eating them.
- Acidic food – e.g. lemon/lime/orange/grapefruit.
- Alcohol.

MAY BE POSITIVE FOR SLEEP:

- A milky drink – milk contains a chemical called tryptophan, an amino acid which helps us produce the chemical serotonin, which in turn has a positive role in sleep. The amounts are so small that the effect is likely to be minimal. However, many people find a milky drink soothing and calming and this can have a psychological benefit for sleep.

- A small carbohydrate-based snack (as long as not too sugary) – while unlikely to make you sleepy directly, a light carb-based snack can help tryptophan do its job. Perhaps an unsweetened digestive biscuit or a couple of oatcakes with your milk?

- A herbal tea – many herbs are helpful for sleep, including chamomile, hops, passiflora (passion flower) and valerian. Again, even if the biological effect of a tea isn't huge it's psychologically calming.

- Having a small snack to avoid being hungry – something easy to digest and bland, such as a cheese sandwich. Include some protein in your snack. As well as milk, the following protein-based foods are relatively high in tryptophan: turkey, chicken, eggs, fish, cheese, peanuts, beans, nuts and seeds. (Again, the actual level of tryptophan will be very small but a small snack that incorporates some protein can still be helpful for sleep.)

- There are other foods for which a decent amount of research suggests that they might at least be worth including in your evening diet: Kiwi fruit; nuts, especially almonds, Brazil nuts and walnuts; sour cherry juice; lettuce, especially romaine; oily fish such as salmon. **But it's not sensible to overload on any one food because if you do you risk creating a lack of balance. Eat a wide variety of things because no single food is The Magic One.**

SUPER-CHARGED SLEEP WARNING
DON'T TAKE SUPPLEMENTS FOR TRYPTOPHAN

The safe way to obtain the right levels of this amino acid is to eat a varied diet that includes the foods mentioned above. Too much of tryptophan can have significant unpleasant side effects.

SUPER-CHARGED SLEEP QUESTION
IF LARGE MEALS ARE BAD FOR SLEEP, WHY DO WE OFTEN FEEL SO SLEEPY AFTER A LARGE MEAL, ESPECIALLY THANKSGIVING, CHRISTMAS OR OTHER FEAST?

Yes, we often feel sleepy and even nod off after a large meal but we don't sleep long, deeply or well. We are likely to wake up soon after and feel drowsy, groggy and possibly nauseous. So, feasts make us sleepy but don't lead to a healthy night-time sleep.

Some people have linked sleepiness after a traditional Thanksgiving or Christmas meal to eating turkey, because turkey is known to contain tryptophan. But it's much more likely to be the sleepiness from a large meal, rather than turkey specifically.

SUPER-BUSTED SLEEP MYTH
CHEESE GIVES YOU BAD DREAMS

It doesn't! This myth has probably grown from the fact that often people eat cheese at the end of a big meal, usually a heavy, rich meal that they don't digest properly. This can lead to an unsettled night and the likelihood of waking often and remembering dreams.

SPACE YOUR MEALS AND HAVE A ROUTINE

If you eat very little during the day you're likely to feel very hungry in the evening and may eat a large meal that can stop you sleeping well. Spread your food intake out in three moderate meals and have a small snack later in the evening if necessary. Having a routine to your meals is also helpful in regulating your circadian rhythms so that your suprachiasmatic nucleus triggers the melatonin at the time you want to sleep. You can even bring your sleep time earlier by bringing your evening meal earlier.

MAGNESIUM

There's good evidence that having a decent amount of magnesium in our diets can be helpful for natural healthy sleep patterns. Our bodies don't produce magnesium so we can only get it from food. Foods high in magnesium include:

- Avocadoes.
- Nuts – especially almonds, Brazil nuts and cashews.
- Legumes – not as in the French for "vegetables" but a food family that includes chickpeas, lentils, peas, peanuts and soya beans.
- Tofu – made of soya beans.
- Seeds – including pumpkin.
- Whole grains – e.g. oats, whole wheat, barley.
- Oily fish – especially salmon and mackerel.
- Bananas.
- Dark leaf greens – such as spinach, kale, dark cabbage, sprouts.
- Dark chocolate! Must be dark, though. And best not to eat it in the evening, as it contains caffeine...

CAN WEIGHTED BLANKETS HELP WITH SLEEP?

I admit I was sceptical when I first heard about these but then I investigated and found a great deal of positive research. Weighted blankets are not new: they've been used to help people with conditions such as autism for a long time, because the main role of these blankets is to soothe and comfort. There are many studies into their effectiveness for people who have difficulty sleeping and the results are pretty convincing.

As well as autism, weighted blankets can help people with insomnia, broken or disturbed nights, anxiety and related disorders and, some studies show, even depression. They can both help you sleep and help you feel more relaxed while you're awake.

Why? The suggestion is that because the weight of the blanket is like being firmly touched or hugged, this can reduce the stress hormone cortisol and increase serotonin, which has a role in feelings of contentment. It is also possible that it helps production of oxytocin, which is the hormone associated with being touched or hugged. If the blankets do reduce stress and anxiety, making you feel more relaxed and calm, this would explain how they also help sleep.

The blankets come in different sizes and weights and it's important to choose one that is right for your own size and weight. It can be dangerous to use one that's too heavy.

There are some other dangers to be aware of, mainly from buying "fake" products made with hazardous materials. You should only buy from a company you strongly trust and check that you don't have a medical condition that might make a weighted blanket inadvisable.

I'm afraid they aren't cheap (and if you find one that seems cheap you should question its safety) but it could be something to request for your birthday if you feel that this could help you relax and sleep.

Interestingly – or weirdly – I remember that I used to pile my bed with heavy objects when I was a child. I found it comforting to sleep with a small suitcase on top of me!

CHAPTER NINE:
SUPER SLEEP STRATEGIES

You've learnt how to create the best basis for slipping smoothly into sleep. But everyone will sometimes have nights when all of that isn't enough, those nights when a worry or excitement won't let our mind stop whizzing, when we just don't seem to be able to wind down in the normal way.

This chapter gives you some extra tools for those nights. You still need to follow all the earlier advice but these are extra techniques for you. Make sure you learn them before you need them!

EIGHT TRIED AND TESTED SLEEP STRATEGIES

If you think back to a night where you just lay there unable to sleep, you will probably recall the feeling of your mind just refusing to shut down. It could be a general feeling of alertness or it could be something particular on your mind. Perhaps you were going over and over an upsetting, annoying or worrying thing that happened that day. Perhaps you were worrying about a big event coming up. Maybe you had something difficult going on in your life. You might even have just been imagining something awful happening. Equally, your mind could have been going over something really exciting you'd done that day, something amazing and wonderful. Whatever, it just wouldn't shut down for sleep.

This happens to people at all stages of life and to some people more than others. As a teenager, you may well have the pressure of schoolwork, friends, exams, fears of the future.

Whatever it is, that racing mind can stop you getting to sleep for ages – sometimes even a few hours.

Fortunately, I have strategies! These strategies apply whether you're trying to get to sleep at the start of the night or you wake during the night or in the early hours of the morning.

Most importantly, don't panic or feel anxious. It's really not the end of the world and if you have an exam or something that requires peak performance the next day you'll still have your peak performance because adrenaline will make up for your lost sleep. You will get some hours and that will be enough.

If you're lying awake but still feel quite drowsy, give it a bit longer, but don't lie awake for longer than about 30–40 minutes. Yes, I know: it's hard to tell if you're not allowed to look at your clock but you'll probably have a reasonable sense of the time. If you must look at your clock, do!

After that, choose from the following strategies. You can try whichever you want but I've made suggestions to help guide you to particular choices for particular situations.

STRATEGY 1: GET UP AND DO SOMETHING ELSE

(For when you're feeling wide awake and far from sleep, but you don't have a particular worry or repeated thought.)

Get up and **do something that will tire your mind without raising your heart rate.** This could be reading a book, doing a paper-based puzzle, doing a jigsaw, drawing a picture, writing a poem. Avoid opening a screen and avoid bright lights. I recently wrote all my birthday thank-you letters in the middle of the night when I couldn't sleep because my mind was wired after a public speaking event.

Do this for about half an hour or until you feel sleepy and then go back to bed.

STRATEGY 2: MINDFULNESS

(For when your mind is spinning, with or without worry or negative thoughts.)

Mindfulness – a form of meditation – has become very popular in recent years and it does seem to help some people. It doesn't help everyone, however, so don't feel there's something wrong with you if it doesn't work for you.

Mindfulness is about focusing your thoughts on your body and mind as it is in the present, rather than thinking about the past or future or external things. So typical mindfulness exercises ask you to notice all sorts of feelings in your body and mind, not analysing them or judging or changing them, just noticing.

Mindfulness experts would usually suggest that you practise this during the day, not specifically or only when you're trying to get to sleep. The advantage of practising during the day – or earlier in the evening – is that you can use one of the many mindfulness apps and audio recordings to learn the skills, so that at night you can just do it yourself, without the intrusion of technology. You'll find a useful resource for mindfulness on page 185.

STRATEGY 3: A MENTAL MASSAGE

(For when your mind is spinning, with or without worry or negative thoughts.)

Settle into the most comfortable position you can find and relax your muscles, focusing on the muscles in your neck, jaw, scalp and all the many muscles in your face and around your eyes.

Then **imagine a hand gently on your brain, light as air, softly stroking and soothing your mind.** Imagine yourself feeling nothing physically but sensing the presence of a kindly force that slows down your thoughts, calming them down, settling them, preventing them from wandering. You might imagine your head being softly bandaged in cotton wool or wrapped in warmth or visualise yourself floating in water – anything that makes you focus your thoughts on your brain, head and eyes, the place where sleep begins when thoughts and ideas stop spinning. Imagine it a place of stillness, of peace, comfort, safety and sleep.

This takes a bit of practice but it's a really good way of calming your mind.

STRATEGY 4: CONTROL YOUR PHYSICAL STATE

(For when you're feeling alert and awake, with or without worry or negative thoughts.)

The three things to focus on are: muscles, heart rate and breathing. By focusing on them, you can consciously relax your muscles and slow your heart-rate and breathing, sending your body into a sleepy state. Simultaneously, you'll find that by focusing your mind onto your physical state you will take your mind off any worries or intrusive thoughts.

A useful way to start is to **tense each group of muscles in turn, followed by relaxing them.** So, start with your toes: scrunch them up and then relax them; relax them further; think about this for a few seconds until you've relaxed them as much as you can. Next move to your calf muscles, then your

thigh muscles, buttocks, lower abdomen, stomach, chest –
pause here and think about your breathing, slowing it a little
further, sinking your chest muscles further – then fingers, arms,
shoulders, neck. Spend extra time focusing on each part of your
head: up the back of your skull, over your scalp, forehead, the
muscles around your eyes, cheeks, and finally your jaw. Many
people hold tension in their jaw and it can be really satisfying to
release this tension that you didn't even know was there.

Continue to focus on your breathing, taking it to a slow,
relaxed speed. Don't make your breaths too deep, just nice and
slow, with a little more emphasis on the out breath, feeling your
abdominal muscles soften each time.

Doing all this will slow your heart rate, too, without you
really thinking about it.

STRATEGY 5: VISUALISE YOUR HAPPIEST PLACE

(For when worries go round and round and you can't stop stressing
about them.)

This is a method of directing your thoughts away from any
anxiety patterns or worry loops. It builds a state of calm
but, unlike simple muscle relaxation or breath control, it also
requires so much concentration or "brain bandwidth" that you
can't simultaneously engage in your worries. It's a fundamental
distraction technique to redirect your thoughts.

Here's how it works. **Choose an ideal location, a place
you'd love to be. It could be somewhere familiar, such
as in your garden on a sun-lounger or hammock, or
a place you've been on holiday.** Or it could be a place
you're imagining, such as a tropical island or desert or a log
cabin. You could be lying relaxing or you could be walking

or running, if you enjoy that; you could even be skiing or skateboarding. Wherever you choose, it needs to be where you want to be, where you can feel at your happiest.

Picture yourself there. Build in some details: the temperature, what you're wearing, what you are sitting or lying on – or where you're walking, if that's what you've chosen. What can you see? Trees swaying? Waves rolling? Birds wheeling? Or are your eyes closed? Can you feel the sun on your skin? A breeze in your hair? Any smells – grass, sea, a barbecue, a freshly baked cake, roses, freshly washed sheets? What about sounds: seagulls, crashing waves, wind in the trees, a train, children playing, a dog barking? The more you focus on the detail, the less able your mind is to dwell on your worry.

STRATEGY 6: VISUALISE A JOURNEY

(For when worries go round and round and you can't stop stressing about them.)

This has the same effect as Strategy 5 – it requires concentration, helping shift your thoughts away from worry loops.

Think of a journey you know well. It could be your journey to school or it could be a route around a nearby shopping centre. (Note: if your journey to school is associated with significant negative feelings or anxiety, you might be better not choosing this. Perhaps your journey home from school might work better?) **Simply direct your mind to trace that journey in as much detail as possible, as slowly as possible, thinking of your feet moving one at a time.** Again, build in as much detail as you can: weather, your clothes, things you see.

STRATEGY 7: VISUALISE A STORY WITH YOU AS THE HERO

(For when worries go round and round and you can't stop stressing about them.)

This has the same effect as 5 and 6. It takes a bit longer to start with but is potentially more powerful, as it's extra-engaging. **You'll be creating your perfect daydream, a story where the best things happen to you, where you're the centre of the story.** You can revisit it each night and relive your wonderful story.

Here's how. Think of something you'd love to happen to you. Perhaps there's someone you admire (or fancy!) and you'd love them to notice you being brilliantly successful or strong, perhaps winning a prize or saving someone's life. Perhaps there's a far-off ambition you have – winning an Olympic medal, becoming famous for an amazing achievement, making a speech in front of thousands, being signed by a major record label, being the best in your country at something. It doesn't matter how extreme or unlikely the ambition is but it could equally be something more likely, such as winning a writing or singing competition, or scoring the crucial goal or try for your team.

Now build that story. Add in masses of detail. Focus on your feelings. You can keep going over bits if you want to. You might finish the story and start again or you might not finish it. Maybe tomorrow night you'll do it differently. Each time you do it you will access positive emotions even more and it will be easier and easier. You'll even start to look forward to turning your light off so you can get back to the story where you star!

STRATEGY 8: COUNTING OR NAMING

(A general distraction technique many people use to switch them into sleep mode.)

You'll have heard of counting sheep. Sheep are useful because we can all picture them quite easily and they tend to follow each other so we can imagine them one by one going through a gap in a fence, for example. They tend to stick together, too, so it's not easy to count them. This means that, while it's easy (for most people, although not everyone) to visualise the sheep, it also requires some effort to count them. You can also add in details such as three sheep going through the gap together, or one going back out again or going through the wrong gap or getting stuck. The more detail you can add, the better your mind will focus on these imaginary sheep instead of your worries.

But it doesn't have to be sheep! It could be cats or mice or elephants or anything that moves.

Another counting exercise involves counting backwards from 100. When I do this I generally reach about 89 before I've either fallen asleep or started thinking of something else. However, if you're having a really bad night, this may not be enough and it can be distressing to reach the lower numbers and still not be asleep.

Similarly, there are mental naming activities, such as:

- How many animals/people/countries/whatever can you think of beginning with A (or other letter)?
- Name an animal/person/country beginning with each letter of the alphabet.
- Put the US states or any other list in alphabetical order.
- Play "I went to the shops and bought..." adding one more thing each time.

WHEN YOU NEED MORE HELP

All the strategies above are important to try; if they don't always work you shouldn't ignore them. Just because they didn't work on one or two occasions doesn't mean they won't work another time. They are still good strategies and worth trying. But there are more things to consider if you feel that poor sleep has become a major part of your life and you are becoming distressed by it. First, let's try to work out why.

QUIZ: WHY ARE YOU SLEEPING BADLY?

1. Look at the sleep negatives on page 140 – do any of them feature in your evening?

   a. No.
   b. Sometimes – I'll try to fix this.
   c. Sometimes – but I can't fix them all.

2. Do you have a particular worry, stress or upset going on in your life at the moment?

   a. No.
   b. Yes.

3. Is your sleep harmed by something outside you, such as noise in the house?

   a. No.
   b. Yes.

4. Is your sleep harmed by something inside you, such as worries, anxieties or negative thoughts?

   a. No.
   b. Yes.

5. Does your life make an evening routine really difficult or impossible?

   a. No, I have a good evening routine and get to bed at the right time.
   b. On some nights it's possible but on others it's not.
   c. Yes, I really can't achieve a routine.

6. Do you take a long time to fall asleep?

   a. Not particularly.
   b. Sometimes.
   c. Often or always.

7. Do you wake in the middle of the night and take a long time to get back to sleep?

   a. Not particularly.
   b. Sometimes.
   c. Often or always.

8. Do you wake early in the morning and then not get back to sleep?

   a. Not particularly.
   b. Sometimes.
   c. Often or always.

9. Would you like to go to bed earlier?

    a. I think I go to bed at the right time for me – I'm
       allowing a sleep opportunity of 7–9 hours.
    b. Yes, but I can't because of factors outside
       my control.
    c. Yes, and this is something I could try.

10. Do you feel very tired during the day?

    a. Not particularly.
    b. Sometimes.
    c. Often or always.

WHAT YOUR ANSWERS TELL YOU

Questions 1–5 could reveal some factors contributing to your sleep problems. Which can you change? How about discussing this with an adult or good friend to see if they can suggest something that hasn't occurred to you? Sometimes we get ourselves into a "I can't change this" mentality when in fact there is something and it may need someone else to help us see it.

Questions 6–8 don't give you clues to a solution but if you've answered c) to question 6 or 7, and if this has been going on for longer than a couple of weeks and is making you worried or unwell, I recommend you consult a doctor so that a cause such as low mood or a form of depression can be discounted. See page 107 for sleep and depression.

Question 9 looks at whether your bedtime is early enough and, if not, why not – is it in your control or out of your control? If you think you'd be better going to bed earlier, is there anything at all you can do to help that happen? It's obviously impossible to get enough sleep if you don't find the right "sleep opportunity", but just adding a little bit more can make a noticeable difference.

If you do want to sleep earlier and there are things you can do to achieve this, focus on shifting your bedtime by a small amount (twenty minutes, for example) at first. Simply start your routine earlier.

Question 10 – if you answered a), perhaps you actually are getting enough sleep? Even knowing this can be enough to stop you worrying. If you answered b), it doesn't sound as though you have too big a problem and I predict that your sleep will improve in its own time, if you follow all this book's advice. If you answered c), then, yes, this suggests that you are suffering from lack of sleep and better nights are an important goal for you. Try the extra strategies under Strategies When Sleep Problems Persist.

Your sleep problems are most likely to be caused by any (or all) of these: too many sleep negatives during your evening, a worry or stress, external factors such as noise, or not giving yourself enough sleep opportunity. Once you think you know what the problems are, you can see what strategies might help best.

STRATEGIES WHEN SLEEP PROBLEMS PERSIST

First, re-read and make sure you fully appreciate the whole section on sleep hygiene, routines and strategies from page 133. All the advice that follows assumes that you are doing absolutely everything I've already suggested!

KEEP A SLEEP DIARY

Even if you know all the sleep positives and negatives and are following them as well as you can, it's not possible to get it right every time. There may be something you're doing without noticing that it has a negative effect for you. Keeping a sleep diary for a couple of weeks is the best way to enable you to spot what this might be. Remember there's a template on page 18.

Also, if you go to a doctor or sleep expert about the problem, this is one of the first things they will ask for.

TRY A DIFFERENT ROUTINE

You've already got a routine, as I advised on page 142, haven't you? Maybe it's not working and you need a new start. Perhaps you could create a new one? A bigger, more interesting one, something with a more noticeable element to it? Perhaps there could always be a bath with lavender oil just before you get into bed? Perhaps you could create a special playlist for sleep and only play it at this time?

Do your new routine for five days, while also keeping a sleep diary. Do you notice any change? If not, a few more days could be the answer. Sometimes brains create habits quickly but sometimes they need a bit more time.

SUPER-CHARGED SLEEP QUESTION
WHAT ABOUT HERBAL REMEDIES?

Herbal sleeping pills are not generally a good idea because there's a chance that, if they work, you'll want to keep using them and it could be hard to stop. However, if you are having genuine difficulty and your poor sleep is becoming distressing, or you have a particular reason for needing your best sleep tonight, there's not really a good reason why you shouldn't use a herbal remedy very occasionally. However, these are very important rules:

- If you take any other medication, whether from your doctor or bought over the counter, check with a doctor or qualified pharmacist that there's no reason not to take a herbal remedy you're considering.
- Only buy from a reputable pharmacy or health food shop.
- Never exceed the recommended dose.
- Never take two different remedies together.
- Don't take more than two nights in a row.
- If your sleep problems continue, see a doctor and do mention that you tried these remedies.

SEE A DOCTOR OR OTHER MEDICAL EXPERT

Sometimes, seeing a doctor is the sensible thing to do. Times when I'd recommend this would be:

- If you have tried as many of the strategies in this book as you can and they don't seem to be working. You should try them for at least two weeks.
- If you are feeling really unwell and unable to function properly on a daily basis.
- If you think you have symptoms of depression or other mental illness.
- If you have any other reason to worry.

What might the doctor do? First, they would ask you lots of questions to point them towards what was going on. They would probably ask you to keep a sleep diary. So, if you've done this already, take it with you. They will also make sure you know all the good healthy advice – tell them you've read this book!

Then, depending on what they thought the problem might be, they would give you advice and perhaps refer you to a sleep clinic. They might also discuss any of the following treatment options.

SLEEPING PILLS

Sleeping pills are not advisable except in a few very specific circumstances and only under expert guidance. A doctor might prescribe them for a short period to someone going through grief or other exceptional anxiety caused by a difficult event. This kind of medication would be appropriate for "acute" (sudden, specific and short-term) sleeping problems but not for "chronic" (long-term) ones. **Never buy sleeping pills online. Never take a sleeping pill prescribed for someone else.**

Sleeping pills carry a high risk of addiction and dependency and can also make you feel groggy the next day. Sleeping pills also don't produce normal sleep architecture. Compared to a typical pattern, a pill-induced sleep is likely to be different in terms of the time spent in each stage. Biology gives us the type of sleep we need; pills can counteract that.

If your doctor believes you need sleeping pills, they will talk you through it. It's very important to follow your doctor's advice. They not only know about medicines but they also know you.

MELATONIN

You've learnt about melatonin, the naturally-occurring hormone that regulates sleep. But a version is also artificially created to treat certain sleep disorders. You should never take this unless prescribed by a doctor. Melatonin is very rarely prescribed for young people and only with expert supervision. There are possible risks to mental and physical health and the benefits are not as clear as some people think.

Melatonin doesn't make us sleepy. It only helps regulate our circadian rhythms if they have been knocked out of step. What keeps most people awake is an over-alert mind and melatonin doesn't help that.

There are two main situations where melatonin might be prescribed: first, to help prevent jet lag after long-haul air travel. Taking melatonin at carefully calculated times can help avoid this. Second, if someone has been diagnosed with a disorder that means their body clock isn't working properly, so their sleep-wake cycle doesn't match normal hours of darkness and waking. Melatonin may then be prescribed but only with caution.

Adults may also be prescribed melatonin in certain situations involving shift work. And there are some other medical conditions where melatonin can help.

Melatonin has more effects than regulating sleep patterns. We simply don't know enough about negative side effects. The fact that it's possible to buy it without prescription doesn't mean it's safe.

Only ever take melatonin (or any sleep medication) when prescribed by a doctor or in a special sleep clinic. The doctor will give you detailed instructions about when and for how long to take it. Follow the instructions closely. Never take anything prescribed for someone else, even if you think your symptoms are the same.

COGNITIVE BEHAVIOURAL THERAPY FOR INSOMNIA (CBT-I)

CBT-I is a well-established therapy for insomnia which has a lot of research to support it. Looking at over 100 studies, it has about a 70 per cent success rate. CBT-I is what most people should be offered if they have a diagnosis of insomnia that is not related specifically to something dramatic such as bereavement. (It could also be useful in bereavement but it's likely that in these cases the sufferer has enough on their plate without taking on board the hard but effective work of CBT-I.)

If you've heard of normal CBT, you may know that it's a talking therapy that addresses negative and unhelpful thoughts, emotions and behaviours. It can treat anxiety, social anxiety, phobias, panic attacks, some disordered eating, body hatred, self-consciousness and many other ways in which our brains behave unhelpfully or develop negative habits.

CBT-I is therapy directed at negative sleep patterns. It tends to be more practical than normal CBT and usually involves keeping a weekly diary, learning what impedes sleep and what helps it, and building a new set of habits to create a healthy approach to sleep. CBT-I is not a quick fix but it is risk-free. You can't become addicted to it and it can't do you harm or make your sleeping problems worse.

In essence, what you'll learn or do in CBT-I sessions is based on what you've learnt in Chapter Eight. But sometimes habits are so deep-set that you need someone to help unpick them all and reinstate good ones. For example, you might have a strong habit of napping in the evening. It might be really obviously unhelpful but it equally might be difficult to break that negative routine without help.

An expert can give you a gradual programme to change your patterns. For some people, this might even mean at first having less sleep than before – "sleep restriction" – which would be very difficult to feel confident about without expert guidance.

So, yes, even when we know what to do we sometimes need help to make that happen. A therapist can help by being an encouraging, confident voice in your ear. They can also look at your exact situation and suggest changes you could make that you might not have considered. They are not just another pair of eyes but an expert pair of eyes.

Depending on where you live, you might be able to access CBT-I free. There are also online programmes, some of which are free. You'll find some guidance in the CBT-I resources listed on page 184 but a reliable place to start is to ask at your GP practice.

So, sleep hygiene and all my advice up to this point are extremely important and worth trying for everyone; but for some people expert extra help may be needed.

AND FINALLY, TO SLEEP...

You now know all you need to know about sleep! All the wonderful benefits it brings to your mind and body, to your mental and emotional health and to how well your brain works for you in school, at home and in your social life. You've learnt to put sleep near the top of your priorities. But you're not obsessed about it: you know it won't be perfect every night. When it isn't, you don't panic and get your duvet in a tangle. You're realistic about the fact that everyone can have sleepless phases, that lying awake with spiralling thoughts is part of being a thinking, sensitive, creative human and more so for some than others or at some stages of life than others. You have sensible, healthy, proven strategies to call on when those bad nights come. You can even teach the adults in your life how they can sleep better, feel better, function better.

You now have the power to be in as much control as possible of that awesome, fascinating, universal activity that occupies around a third of our lives. Tonight, I guarantee you, at some unseen moment in the peaceful darkness of your bedroom and the cocoon of your bedclothes, your brilliant brain will naturally and seamlessly switch from awake to asleep, your brainwaves jumping from beta to alpha to theta to delta, cycling through stages of light and deep NREM sleep, diving into the mysterious world of REM-dreaming and back again, and again, and again. And, perhaps, again. All the cells of your body and brain will be bathed in sleep and you will receive all the benefits of nature's medicine without having to do a single thing other than let it happen.

Let it happen. Sleep well!

Testing Your Knowledge Now (p.11) Answers:

1. Rapid Eye Movement.

2. First half.

3. That thing where you're just drifting into sleep but you seem to fall down a step and you suddenly jump awake.

4. A bit colder.

5. No, not as far as we know.

6. Yes, we know some other animals do, although we don't know what their dreams are like. We don't know if they all dream.

7. Yes, most experts say that there is a biological difference, although people may change through their lives if they force themselves to, so there may be a social/habit aspect, too. So there's probably a biological component.

8. No! There's definitely a strong biological element – though screens don't help.

9. No, because adrenaline (the main stress chemical) will keep you alert and functioning well. Sleeping badly one night won't make a huge practical difference.

10. The science suggests that ideally Monday during the day would be best, if you have a choice. This is because a) sleep between learning and recalling helps recall and b) learning late at night is likely to damage your sleep.

11. No.

12. Exercise tends to help night-time sleep as long as it's earlier in the day.

13. No – it is more likely to mean that you are anxious about something.

14. Alcohol; going for a run or other sport; checking your phone messages.

GLOSSARY

Adenosine	Hormone which builds up during the day to cause pressure to sleep.
Biphasic, monophasic or polyphasic sleep	Within a 24-hour period, some creatures seem naturally to have two sleeps (biphasic), others one (monophasic) and others many (polyphasic). There's some disagreement as to whether humans are naturally monophasic, with one natural long night-time sleep, or biphasic, with either a night-time sleep split into two (as some cultures seem to have had) or a night-time sleep and a shorter day-time nap. The fact that some cultures do one or the other doesn't prove that it's "natural", as our habits could also be responding to what our society needs.
Brainwaves	Patterns of electrical activity in the brain, changing according to whether we are awake or asleep and which stage or type of sleep we are in.
Circadian rhythms	The daily pattern of internal changes seen in all animals (and even plants) responding to time of day and night. Some animals, such as owls, naturally wake during darkness (nocturnal behaviour) and others, including

humans, are wired to be awake during daylight hours. Different creatures have different natural sleep needs, length and architecture.

fMRI	functional Magnetic Resonance Imaging – a type of non-invasive scan which shows which brain areas are active in particular mental or physical activities. You have to be in a scanner, which limits the physical situations that can be tested, but you can move some parts of your body and perform any mental action.
Ghrelin	Hormone associated with the feeling of hunger.
Hippocampus	An area of the brain very active in processing information and skills and forming memories, therefore crucial for many types of learning.
Hormone	A type of chemical produced by the body, each regulating different biological states, such as sleep, hunger, growth, puberty, fertility.
Leptin	Hormone associated with feeling full, not needing to eat any more.
Melatonin	Hormone associated with the sleep/wake pattern or circadian rhythms.

NREM sleep	Standing for Non Rapid Eye Movement, these are stages of either light or deep sleep in which brainwaves are much slower and regular than when either awake or dreaming.
Prefrontal cortex	Area at the very front of the brain, often described as the control centre because it's what we use and need to exercise self-control, make decisions based on future consequences more than emotion, perform complex critical thinking, be logical. It's much more developed in humans than any other creature and is the last brain area to finish developing, not doing so until well into our twenties.
REM sleep	Standing for Rapid Eye Movement because our eyes flicker back and forth behind closed lids. This is the stage during which we dream. REM brainwaves look very similar to awake brainwaves, but voluntary muscles are paralysed so we don't act out our dreams.
Sleep architecture	How your night breaks down between the various stages and cycles of wake, light NREM, deep NREM and REM sleep.
Sleep latency	How long it takes to fall asleep.

Sleep length	Actual time spent asleep during sleep opportunity.
Sleep opportunity	Total maximum possible sleep time, measured from turning light off to time of needing to wake up.
Sleep spindles	Special brainwaves signifying that we are entering and then remaining in deeper NREM sleep.

RESOURCES

These resources offer starting points or are things I think you might find interesting. There are lots of resources on my website. Go to www.nicolamorgan.com and see the page dedicated to this book or put "sleep" in the search facility.

BEST BOOKS

Night School by Richard Wiseman
Why We Sleep by Matthew Walker
Dreamland – Adventures in the Strange Science of Sleep by David K. Randall

BEST ONLINE

General Facts about sleep: www.ninds.nih.gov/Disorders/Patient-Caregiver-Education/Understanding-Sleep

Sleep myths: www.bbc.co.uk/news/health-47937405

Detail of sleep development, including through adolescence. Loads of references. Also sleep disorders and snoring, restless leg syndrome and depression: www.ncbi.nlm.nih.gov/pmc/articles/PMC3119585/

Sleep pressure/drive: www.howsleepworks.com/how_homeostasis.html

Your country's major health organisations or charities will usually provide the most reliable information. For example:
UK NHS – www.nhs.uk – search "sleep" or more specific topic such as "insomnia"
US – The Sleep Foundation: www.sleepfoundation.org/
Australia – The Sleep Health Foundation:

www.sleephealthfoundation.org.au/

Sleep stages and cycles
Description of stages and cycles: www.livescience.com/59872-stages-of-sleep.html

Images of brainwaves and description of different stages: www.helpguide.org/harvard/biology-of-sleep-circadian-rhythms-sleep-stages.htm

Deep sleep helps clean waste: www.sciencedaily.com/releases/2019/02/190227173111.htm

Possible ways to increase deep sleep: www.healthline.com/health/how-much-deep-sleep-do-you-need#increasing-deep-sleep

Amount of sleep/effects of too little
Useful general article about amounts of sleep: www.theatlantic.com/magazine/archive/2017/01/how-to-sleep/508781/

How long can you go without sleep: www.medicalnewstoday.com/articles/324799.php#how-long-can-you-go-without-sleep

How much sleep do you need: www.sciencefocus.com/the-human-body/michael-mosley-how-much-sleep-do-you-really-need/

Gene for needing little sleep: www.ucsf.edu/news/2019/08/415261/after-10-year-search-scientists-find-second-short-sleep-gene

Sleep deprivation (includes information about other animals): www.ncbi.nlm.nih.gov/pmc/articles/PMC2525690/

Specific benefits of sleep
Sleep and athletic performance: http://eujsm.eu/index.php/
EUJSM/article/download/53/14

Sleep linked to academic grades: www.sleepforscience.org/
stuff/contentmgr/files/52a3d7d8fccfd8d14eb35108b5ef8f67/
pdf/wolfson_carskadonsmr2003.pdf

Teenage sleep
Teenage brain patterns: www.pbs.org/wgbh/pages/frontline/
shows/teenbrain/from/sleep.html

Adolescent sleep patterns and daytime sleepiness: www.ncbi.
nlm.nih.gov/books/NBK222804/

Research into health habits in Scotland; teenage girls sleeping
less; sleep deprivation affects older girls' mental health most:
www.bbc.co.uk/news/uk-scotland-51302485

WHO study 2020 into teenagers getting too little sleep:
www.bbc.co.uk/news/education-51207415

Insomnia and strategies for better sleep
UK NHS advice: www.nhs.uk/live-well/sleep-and-tiredness/
how-to-get-to-sleep/

American Sleep Association – insomnia causes: www.
sleepassociation.org/sleep-disorders/insomnia/insomnia-
causes/

WebMD tips: www.webmd.com/women/guide/insomnia-tips

CBT-I: www.sleepfoundation.org/articles/cognitive-behavioral-

Zzz

therapy-insomnia
https://en.wikipedia.org/wiki/Cognitive_behavioral_therapy_
for_insomnia#Stimulus_control

Magnesium: https://thesleepdoctor.com/2017/11/20/
magnesium-effects-sleep/

Mindfulness for sleep - Headspace: www.headspace.com/
meditation/sleep
www.nosleeplessnights.com/mindfulness-exercises/

Too Much Sleep / Narcolepsy
www.1stopsnoring.co.uk/sleep-conditions/narcolepsy/

www.narcolepsy.org.uk/about-narcolepsy

Hypersomnia: www.hypersomniafoundation.org/

Lucid dreaming
www.medicalnewstoday.com/articles/323077.php#1

https://thesleepdoctor.com/2019/02/26/are-you-a-lucid-
dreamer/

Night terrors
www.nhs.uk/conditions/night-terrors/

Sleepwalking
www.sleepfoundation.org/articles/sleepwalking

Social media use and poor sleep
Focusing on teenagers: https://thesleepdoctor.
com/2019/09/01/social-media-teenagers-lack-of-sleep/

Larks or owls

https://sleepcouncil.org.uk/sleep-hub/are-you-an-owl-or-a-lark/

Animals and sleep

https://video.nationalgeographic.com/video/news/0000014f-9a24-dd5e-a75f-bf64a8a60000

ENDNOTES

[1] Referred to in Matthew Walker's *Why We Sleep* Chapter 8

[2] www.sleepfoundation.org/articles/lack-sleep-increases-your-risk-some-cancers

[3] https://thesleepdoctor.com/2018/04/10/sleep-deprivation/

[4] Matthew Walker's *Why We Sleep* Chapter 1

[5] www.bbc.com/future/article/20150706-the-woman-who-barely-sleeps

[6] Research by David Dinges and Dr Mark Rosekind reported in www.tuftandneedle.com/resources/when-is-national-nap-day/

[7] https://www.danpink.com/resource/when-larks-owls-and-third-birds/

[8] BBC quiz: https://www.bbc.co.uk/cbbc/quizzes/are-you-a-morning-person-or-night-owl

[9] http://news.mit.edu/2002/dreams

[10] Erin J. Wamsley & Robert Stickgold: www.ncbi.nlm.nih.gov/pmc/articles/PMC3079906/

[11] www.standard.co.uk/lifestyle/why-do-we-dream-matthew-walker-explores-the-theories-behind-nocturnal-fantasias-a3799396.html

[12] This article has a huge amount of information on many effects of sleep deprivation: www.ncbi.nlm.nih.gov/pmc/articles/PMC6143346/

[13] "Oblivescence during sleep and waking" American Journal of Psychology (1924)

[14] "The National Institute of Mental Health Power Nap Study" in 2002

[15] www.narcolepsy.org.uk/sites/narcolepsy.org.uk/files/files/Epworth%20Sleepiness%20Scale.pdf

[16] https://www.ncbi.nlm.nih.gov/pmc/articles/PMC3181883/

[17] Sigmund Freud, *The Interpretation of Dreams*

[18] One study in Germany gave 51% having done it once (https://www.ncbi.nlm.nih.gov/pubmed/21466083?dopt=Abstract) but a large study in Brazil gave a figure of over 75%

[19] 1988, Snyder & Gackenback

ACKNOWLEDGEMENTS

Thanks to my dream team at Walker Books who stayed wide awake throughout. Especially my editor, Alice Primmer, and commissioning editor, Denise Johnstone-Burt, for their ability to see the big picture and small details equally clearly, designer, Laurissa Jones, and cover artist, Thy Bui, for making the book look so gorgeous inside and out.

ALSO BY NICOLA MORGAN:

Zzzzz

zzzz

zzzzz

zzzzz

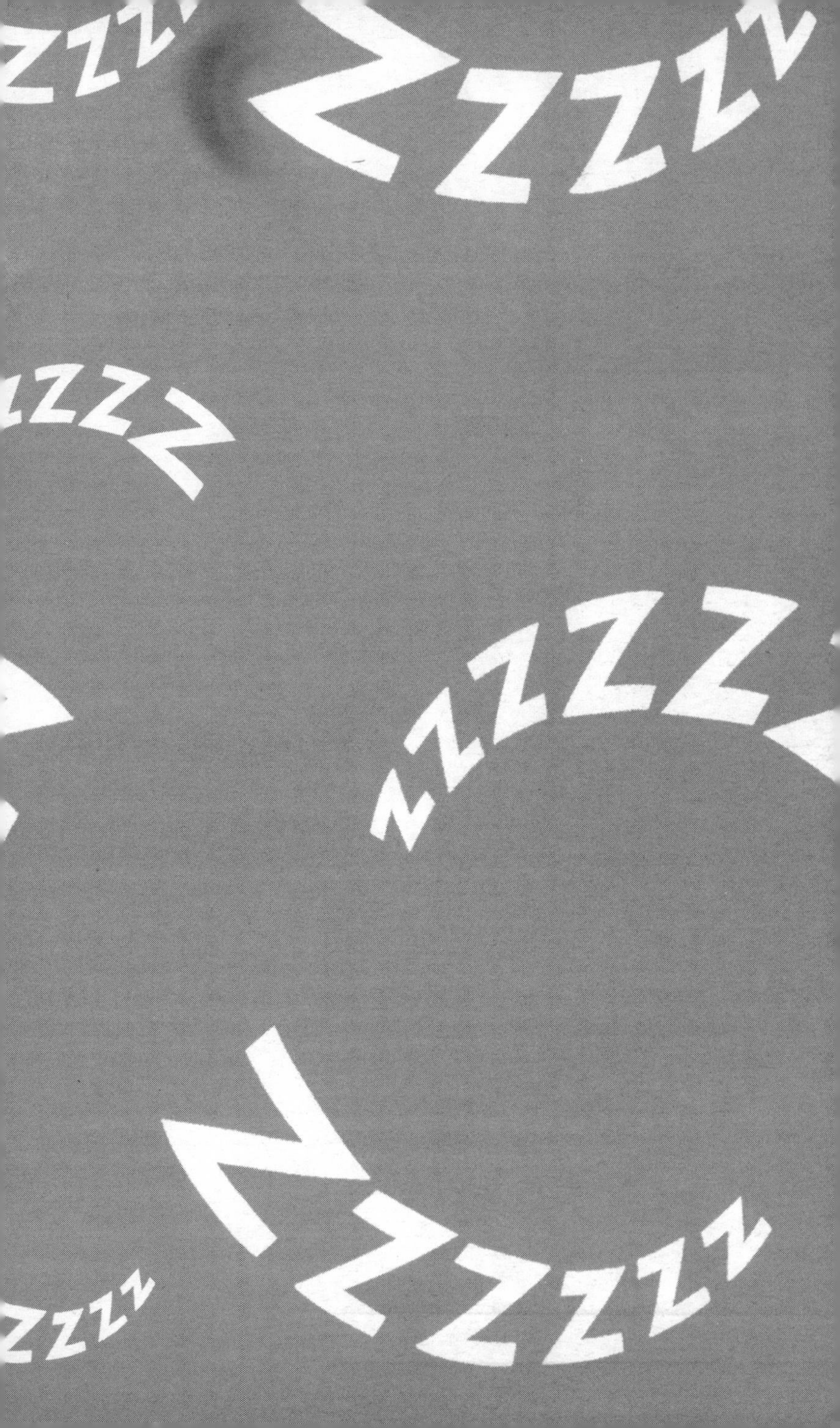